your wedding

linda magistris

For over 60 years, more than 50 million people have learnt over 750 subjects the **teach yourself** way, with impressive results.

be where you want to be
with **teach yourself**

For UK order enquiries: please contact Bookpoint Ltd, 130 Milton Park, Abingdon, Oxon, OX14 4SB. Telephone: +44 (0) 1235 827720. Fax: +44 (0) 1235 400454. Lines are open 09.00–17.00, Monday to Saturday, with a 24-hour message answering service. Details about our titles and how to order are available at www.teachyourself.co.uk

For USA order enquiries: please contact McGraw-Hill Customer Services, PO Box 545, Blacklick, OH 43004-0545, USA. Telephone: 1-800-722-4726. Fax: 1-614-755-5645.

For Canada order enquiries: please contact McGraw-Hill Ryerson Ltd, 300 Water St, Whitby, Ontario, L1N 9B6, Canada. Telephone: 905 430 5000. Fax: 905 430 5020.

Long renowned as the authoritative source for self-guided learning – with more than 50 million copies sold worldwide – the **teach yourself** series includes over 500 titles in the fields of languages, crafts, hobbies, business, computing and education.

British Library Cataloguing in Publication Data: a catalogue record for this title is available from the British Library.

Library of Congress Catalog Card Number: on file.

First published in UK 2007 by Hodder Education, 338 Euston Road, London, NW1 3BH.

First published in US 2007 by The McGraw-Hill Companies, Inc.

This edition published 2007.

Typeset by Transet Limited, Coventry, England.
Printed in Great Britain for Hodder Education, a division of Hodder Headline, an Hachette Livre UK Company, 338 Euston Road, London, NW1 3BH, by Cox & Wyman Ltd, Reading, Berkshire.

Impression number 10 9 8 7 6 5 4 3 2 1
Year 2010 2009 2008 2007

contents

introduction		**xi**
01	**the preliminaries**	**1**
	the engagement	2
	choosing your bridal party	4
	speeches	9
	who pays for what?	10
	seating plans	11
	receiving line	12
	stag and hen parties	13
02	**the planning**	**15**
	how? when? where? how much?	16
	weddings on a budget	17
	wedding planners	17
	choosing the day	19
	the itinerary	21
	year planner	21
	wedding shows	25
	booking suppliers	27
	checking and double-checking	28
	insurance	28
	health and fitness	30
	bridal magazines	31
	stress busters	31
03	**the formalities**	**32**
	civil or church ceremony?	33
	church of England	33
	catholic church	35

	preparation classes	37
	bible readings	37
	alternative bible readings	39
	grace	40
	civil ceremonies	41
	readings for a civil ceremony	42
	commissioning a poem	46
	civil partnerships	46
	humanist blessing	49
	second marriages	49
	marrying abroad	50
	combining a wedding abroad with a church blessing	52
	marrying a foreign national	52
	asian weddings	53
04	**venues**	**55**
	a crucial decision	56
	questions to ask the management at the venue	56
	city weddings	58
	country weddings	60
	scottish weddings	61
	sources of information for venues	61
	marquee weddings	63
	the weather	65
	wedding venues abroad	66
05	**styling/personalizing your wedding**	**71**
	choosing your theme	72
	proficient professionals or determined DIY?	74
	illuminating your day	75
	table tops and co-ordinating chairs	77
	chic crockery and gorgeous glassware	78
	perfect place settings	79
	the seating plan	79
	unique place cards	79

	confetti	80
	favours	81
	balloon decoration	83
	happy snaps	84
	impressive ice	84
	enchanting entrance	84
06	**stationery and gift lists**	**85**
	the invitations	86
	save the date cards	86
	what to include on the invitation	87
	civil partnership invitations	87
	evening invitations	88
	reply cards	88
	thank you cards	88
	order of service	88
	order of the day	88
	place cards	88
	menus	89
	seating plan	89
	guest books	89
	stationery on a budget	89
	gift lists	90
	charity gift lists	91
	alternative gifts	92
07	**wedding attire**	**93**
	bridal wear	94
	menswear	101
	asian wear	103
08	**catering**	**104**
	meeting the caterer	105
	the modern palate	105
	special dietary requirements	106
	organic excellence	109
	advantages of a corporate hotel	110
	wedding packages	112

	drinks	114
	the wedding cake	116
	chocolate fountains	119
	champagne/wine fountains	120
	chocolates and after dinner novelties	120
09	**the flowers**	**122**
	choosing your florist	123
	what to look out for	123
	bridal bouquets	124
	flowers for the bridal party	125
	the meanings of flowers	126
	reception flowers	128
	gifts for the mother of the bride/groom	128
	wedding cake flowers	128
	throwing the bouquet	129
	bouquet preservation	129
	ideas for fun flower arrangements	129
	flowers on a budget	130
	seasonal flowers	131
	confetti	132
	car flowers	133
10	**photographs/video**	**134**
	choosing a photographer	135
	things to check	136
	new styles in wedding photography	137
	modern wedding photography	138
	post-production	139
	fees	139
	list of shots	140
	presentation of the photographs	140
	videos	141
11	**the entertainment**	**144**
	bands	145
	discotheques	146
	agencies	146

	booking the artist	148
	marvellous music!	149
	church music	151
	music for the ceremony	154
	catholic wedding music	156
	civil ceremony music	156
	alternative/additional entertainment	158
	entertaining children at a wedding	158
	firework displays	159
12	**wedding transport**	**161**
	cars	162
	checklist of questions to ask your car supplier	164
	horse and carriage	164
	unusual transport	165
	transport on a budget	167
13	**first night stays**	**169**
	where to stay on your wedding night	170
	fabulous honeymoon destinations	171
	honeymoon countdown	173
	packing your suitcase	176
14	**happily ever after**	**178**
	returning home	179
	changing your name	179
	civil partnership – name change	180
	making a will	180
	your wedding dress – store it or sell it?	182
	the art of compromise	184
	keeping the passion alive!	186
	wedding anniversaries	188
	renewing your vows	189
	finale	190
taking it further		**192**
	useful organizations	192
	useful suppliers	192

dedication

For my mother, Shirley, and my two gorgeous children, Ben and Amy. Thank you for your patience, love and understanding. You are all fantastic!

about the author

Having worked for 18 years as an actress in television, film, theatre and radio, Linda established her successful Wedding Consultancy in 1991, building firm and trusting long-term relationships with both her suppliers and clients.

Her conscientious working practice, great attention to detail, and a fabulous sense of fun, guarantee that every event is a wonderfully stylish and unique experience.

introduction

'One word frees us of all the weight and pain of life. That word is love.'

Sophocles

Many congratulations on your forthcoming marriage! This will be an exciting, thrilling, yet inevitably exhausting journey towards your wedding day, so be prepared – you will need all the help and support your family and friends can provide. Organizing a wedding is an incredibly time-consuming exercise and will occupy many hours, days and weeks of your life. Those who have embarked on arranging this very special event before you have been known to comment on their preconceptions of how simple they thought it was all going to be, until they actually began their preparations and realized what a daunting task was ahead of them. Nevertheless, albeit at times somewhat stressful, this is a wonderfully unique period in your life and one that should be treasured and remembered with joy.

This book aims to eliminate any undue anxiety and pressure for the novice event organizer, providing you with a step-by-step guide to the knowledge you will need to achieve your perfect day, saving you precious time and making the whole process simpler to comprehend. It is packed full of inspirational ideas and exciting new concepts, to help enhance and exceed your highest expectation for the big day. You will be steered carefully through every aspect of wedding planning; with the benefit of a totally comprehensive catalogue of information, advice and Top Tips provided in a logical order, to arm you with a clear understanding of how to proceed with arranging one of the most important days of your life.

A wedding is a fabulously grand party, and probably the most expensive one you will ever host. Therefore it needs careful thought and consideration in order for it to be a successful, memorable and unique event. You will be given the invaluable benefit of hindsight, through my many years of first-hand experience of planning weddings: this will prove vital in preventing any problems and avoiding potential disasters. Above all my aim is to ensure that you experience a great deal of pleasure and fun throughout the planning stages in the months leading up to the big day, culminating in the happiest, most memorable wedding day ever!

Finally, try to remember that although the cake needs to be chosen, the cars booked, the entertainment sorted, and the bride's dream dress fitted, the wedding you are planning is primarily about two people in love who want to share their happiness with family and friends. Often the excitement and nerves of worrying whether every detail of your painstaking work will be fulfilled can overshadow what is really important. That is the moment you say 'I do' and declare your love for your partner; so if you can, stop for a just a second before you say those words, cherish the feelings you both have and savour every second of this wonderful memory that will last forever.

Customs and traditions

A wedding is one of life's primeval and unaffected rites of passage and many of the customs we honour today are simply echoes of the past. The lifting of the veil, flowers, throwing of rice and old shoes, all hold a very particular and significant meaning. With the passing of time, often the original connotation has been forgotten; however we still continue to embody many of the basic customs today.

The word 'wedding', derived from the ancient Greek word 'pledge' and the Anglo-Saxon word 'wedd' – meaning to 'gamble' or 'wager' – meant exactly that! Brides were seen as bargaining tokens, in exchange for land, social status, political alliance, or currency, with the goods being collected by the bride's father.

Here is a brief look at some enduring Western wedding traditions.

The veil

The lifting of the veil has its origins in the bible, from the story of Jacob, who married Leah by mistake, instead of Rachel, the woman he loved. One thought is that as the father of the bride gave her away to the groom, the veil was lifted before the final vows were said, to ensure the groom was getting the bride he had bargained for – quite literally! Originally worn by Roman brides, the veil was also considered to disguise the bride so that evil spirits could not recognize her.

Something old …

Something old,
Something new,
Something borrowed,
Something blue
And a silver sixpence in your shoe.

This rhyme originated in Victorian times, although some of the references are much older.

- **'Something old'** represents the couple's friends, who will hopefully remain close during the marriage. Traditionally, this would be a garter which was given to the bride from a happily married woman, therefore passing on the legacy of her wedded bliss to the new bride.
- **'Something new'** symbolizes the newlyweds' happy and prosperous future (the wedding dress is usually new).
- **'Something borrowed'** is often a much treasured item lent by the bride's family and then returned to them to ensure good luck.
- The tradition of wearing **'something blue'** originated in ancient Israel, where the bride wore a blue ribbon in her hair to represent fidelity, blue being the colour of purity.
- A **'silver sixpence'** was placed in the bride's shoe to ensure wealth in the marriage. Modern brides often substitute a penny for the less common sixpence.

Shoes

It is thought that the Egyptians first introduced shoes to the traditions of a wedding, which were a significant part of their rituals. They exchanged sandals when they traded goods, and when the father of the bride betrothed his daughter to the groom, he would also offer the bride's sandals to show that she now belonged to him. In Anglo-Saxon times, the groom would tap the heel of the bride's shoe to show his authority over her. In later times, shoes were thrown at the couple as a symbol of fertility; thankfully nowadays the shoes are tied to the couple's car instead!

To 'Tie the knot'

This expression originates from the Romans, whose brides wore a girdle tied in knots allowing the groom to have the fun of unravelling them!

The bride on the left/groom on the right

This tradition has its roots in more bloody times when the groom held his sword in his right hand (to fight off any objecting warriors) and held on to his beloved with his left hand.

The journey to the ceremony

It is thought to bring good luck if the bride takes a last look in a mirror before leaving for the ceremony; however, returning to the mirror once she has begun her journey will result in bad luck!

Seeing a chimney sweep on the way to the ceremony is also supposed to bring good luck. It is still possible to hire a sweep's attendance at a wedding today, which is fortunate as the likelihood of bumping into a Dick Van Dyke look-a-like on the way to the church is pretty remote!

Other good luck omens to see are lambs, toads, spiders, black cats and rainbows; monks and nuns are bad omens, perhaps because they are associated with poverty and chastity.

Bad weather on the way to the wedding is thought to be a sign of an unhappy marriage. However in some cultures rain is considered to be good luck: the Italians have a saying *Sposa bagnata, Sposa fortunata* which translates as 'a wet bride is a lucky bride' – I am not sure if every bride would agree!

Crossing the threshold

Traditionally the groom will carry the bride across the threshold of their new marital home. The background for this custom is uncertain, with several explanations: one is that the bride will encounter bad luck if she falls as she goes in; another is that the bride will be unlucky if she walks into the new home with her left foot first; a third account is that it symbolizes the old Anglo-Saxon custom of the groom stealing his bride and carrying her off.

Tossing the bouquet and the garter

During the fourteenth century, having a piece of the bride's clothing was thought to bring good fortune and brides used to be left in tatters after guests had pulled at the wedding dress to gain their snippet of cloth and promise of good luck. In order to prevent this unpleasant ritual, brides retaliated by throwing items at the guests, one of which was the garter belt. Today's bride keeps the garter if she has one and instead has replaced it with her bouquet, which is tossed to the single women in the party – with whoever catches it said to be the next person to marry.

Choosing the day

Sunday used to be the most popular wedding day, as it was the one day most people were free from work. However, Puritans in the seventeenth century put a stop to this, believing it was improper to be festive on the Sabbath. Today Saturday is always the busiest day for nuptials.

The season to marry

The saying 'Marry in the month of May and you'll live to rue the day' dates back to Pagan times when May (being the start of summer) was traditionally pledged to outdoor orgies: for example, the summer festival of Beltane.

Queen Victoria is said to have banned her children from marrying in May and nineteenth century vicars were rushed off their feet on April 30th because brides refused to marry during May. The rhyme goes:

Married when the year is new, he'll be loving kind and true.
When February birds do mate, you wed nor dread your fate.
If you wed when March winds blow, joy and sorrow both you'll know.
Marry in April when you can, Joy for Maiden and for Man.
Marry in the month of May, and you'll surely rue the day.
Marry when June roses grow, over land and sea you'll go.
Those who in July do wed, must labour for their daily bread.
Whoever wed in August be, many a change is sure to see.
Marry in September's shrine, your living will be rich and fine.
If in October you do marry, love will come but riches tarry.
If you wed in bleak November, only joys will come, remember.
When December snows fall fast, marry and true love will last.

The wedding ring

Wearing a wedding ring on the third finger symbolizes marriage, as the Egyptians believed that a vein ran directly from the third finger to the heart. It also signifies the Holy Trinity '... in the name of the Father, the Son and the Holy Ghost'.

The ring has been a symbol of marriage since the Egyptian era with its circular shape representing unending love. Some cultures took it as a symbol of ownership, for it was a token given to the bride to show that the groom owned her.

The ceremonial first kiss

This is the emblematic exchange of spirit as each new spouse breathes a part of their soul into the other. This is why it is important for the groom to be the first to kiss his bride.

Cultural traditions

Africa

The tradition of 'Jumping the Broom' dates back to the times of slavery when African Americans were not allowed to formally marry and set up home together. In a public declaration of unity, they both jumped over a broom into the 'marriage', symbolizing the start of homemaking for the newly 'wed' couple.

Shell necklaces made from smooth Cowrie shells were worn to encourage fertility and were thought to represent beauty and power.

Bermuda

The islanders top their tiered wedding cakes with a tiny sapling that the newlyweds then plant at home, where they can watch it grow with their marriage.

China

The colour red is the favourite for Chinese weddings, bringing luck to the bride. It is used in many forms such as the dress, gift boxes and money envelopes presented to the couple.

Germany

To mark their betrothal, a German couple would give each other gold bands, which are worn on their left hands and throughout their engagement they are referred to as bride and bridegroom.

During the ceremony, when the couple kneel, the groom may kneel on the hem of the bride's dress to show that he will keep her in line, although the bride may step on his foot when she rises, to assert herself – which is only fair!

Greece

On her wedding day a Greek bride carries a lump of sugar in her glove, to be sure of a 'sweet life'.

Ireland

A rich fruit cake, soaked in brandy or bourbon, is the traditional wedding cake of the Emerald Isle. A lucky horseshoe is given to the bride and groom to keep in their home.

Israel

At the end of the ceremony, one of the most dramatic moments in a Jewish marriage is the smashing of the glass by the *Chatan*, which has a variety of explanations. One is that the shattering of glass signals to the ushers to begin the merriment, immediately following the pronouncement of *mazel tov* (congratulations)! Another is that the breaking symbolizes the destruction of the temple in Jerusalem. It also reminds us of the fragility of personal relationships and that the marriage should always remain intact. Finally, the action of the glass being broken by the groom is sometimes explained as representative of the breaking of the bride's hymen, with some modern couples preferring to break the glass together.

The *chupah* (*hoopah*) – the wedding canopy – is usually made of fabric with four corners attached to four poles and stretched over the couple. It is a sign of God's presence and represents a couple's new home.

Japan

On her wedding day, the bride and her family visit the groom's house. She traditionally wears a triangular band on her head, known as the *tsunokakushi*, or horn cover, to hide the horns of jealousy, which reputedly all women possess!

Norway

Two small fir trees are set on either side of the door to the couple's house until they are blessed with a child.

Russia

After a couple are crowned in a Russian Orthodox ceremony, they race to stand on a white rug as it believed that whoever steps on it first, will be the master of the household.

Sweden

The father of the bride gives her a silver coin to place in her left shoe, and a gold coin from her mother is put in her right shoe, so she will never go without. Traditionally the shoes are left unfastened to represent easy childbirth in the future. Wives wear three wedding rings, for betrothal, marriage and motherhood.

the preliminaries

In this chapter you will learn:

- **wedding etiquette**
- **how to choose your bridal party and their roles**
- **who pays for what**
- **how to arrange seating plans**
- **ideas for stag and hen parties.**

The engagement

In the Anglo-Saxon era the engagement period was the time during which the groom took ownership of the bride he had 'stolen' from her father. He was required to pay a 'bride price', as the father of the bride had not only lost a member of his family, but more importantly to him, a valuable worker!

Many centuries later, this tradition was reversed, as the bride's father was then expected to pay a dowry to the groom's family; it was during the engagement period that the bride was able to collect all the items she would take with her into the new marriage (her *trousseau*).

Traditionally men have proposed to women. However, in today's modern society it has become acceptable for women to take the lead and be the ones who instigate a romantic proposal, particularly when the man is dragging his feet and does not seem to show any signs of making the first move! Custom has it that this should only be done on the last day of February in a leap year, but many women now waive this rule and pop the question whenever and wherever they want.

The question has been asked and an affirmative answer given; now is the time for the fun to begin! Initially your family and friends will be informed and then it is time to tell the world, traditionally by placing an announcement in the local or national press.

Announcement example:

C. A. SIMPSON AND MISS G. ROSE

The engagement is announced between Charles,
son of Mr and Mrs Simpson,
and
Georgina, daughter of Mr and Mrs Rose.

It is at this stage that you may consider sending 'Save the date' cards (see Chapter 06 for more details).

Engagement photographs

Many wedding photographers offer engagement photo sessions within their portfolios.

If you have already chosen a photographer for your wedding, an engagement session is a worthwhile exercise for two reasons: firstly, to acquire a memorable set of photographs at an exciting period in the run up to your wedding; secondly it allows you to get to know the person who will be taking your wedding photographs and therefore feel more at ease with him or her on the day.

Rings

The Romans introduced the engagement ring and after they converted to Christianity, a ninth century Pope deemed that engagement rings (or betrothal rings) must be worn. Some couples choose to break from tradition and opt for a more unusual engagement ring, made from a gemstone which represents the birthstone of the bride-to-be. Monthly birthstones are:

Month	Birthstone	Symbolizes
January	garnet	constancy
February	amethyst	sincerity
March	aquamarine, bloodstone	courage
April	diamond	innocence
May	emerald	love, success
June	pearl, alexandrite moonstone	health, longevity
July	ruby	contentment
August	peridot, sardonyx	married happiness
September	sapphire	clear thinking
October	opal, tourmaline	hope
November	topaz	fidelity
December	turquoise, zircon	prosperity

Top tip

An engagement period is often the time when you are likely to receive offers of help from close family or friends and it would be advisable to consider these offers wisely. It is wonderful to have Great Aunt Maud saying that she could make the wedding cake and this may suit your arrangements perfectly. However, you may also have your heart set on a five-tier chocolate extravaganza, with cascading cherubs, and perhaps your Aunt would find it difficult to achieve this particular look! You may have a cousin who wants to do your make-up, which is fabulous if she is an experienced make-up artist; however it is always advisable to arrange a full trial, especially if it is a friend or family who is offering, so that you are not disappointed on the day and there are no awkward feelings between you.

Choosing your bridal party

This is a very exciting time, when you will sit down with your partner and discuss who should play which part in the bridal party. The roles of each member are dictated by etiquette.

Best man

The term 'best man' derives from Scotland, where the bridegroom would 'kidnap' the woman he intended to marry; the toughest of his friends was picked to assist him in the ritual, known as the 'best man'.

The best man has a huge variety of roles, both before the wedding and especially on the day itself.

- Prior to the big day, he should organize the groom's stag night and accompany him and the other members of the male bridal party to their suit fittings.
- He is responsible for ensuring that the groom arrives on time, with his stomach calm and a clear head, and he should guide the ushers in assembling at their correct position in church, or at the civil ceremony.
- The buttonholes are his responsibility and if the florist is not delivering them direct to each member of the bridal party, he should arrange for everyone in the bridal party to receive theirs in good time.

- He should also collect and deliver the Order of Service booklets (if required) to the church or venue.
- The groom looks to the best man for calm reassurance and the guarantee that the ring is safely tucked into a secure suit pocket.
- Once the formalities are over, the best man is in charge of making sure that the guests travel to the reception venue in the correct transport and that they all arrive safely at their destination.
- He should be the liaison between the couple and management of the venue to ensure the smooth running of the day.
- He should ensure that he has some change for gratuities (for example, for the choir or organist) and if any taxis are required, he should deal with the expenses.
- He should arrange that the bride and groom's luggage is taken to the venue if the couple are leaving directly for their honeymoon, along with the receipt of any faxes or telegrams to be used in his speech.
- The best man's speech is always the one that every guest anticipates with great eagerness! To ensure success, it should be warm and humorous, without any embarrassing anecdotes from the groom's bachelor days. It is best that the speech is prepared well in advance, with additions made to it when relevant thoughts occur, so that there is no panic on the day, nor the need for last minute alterations. Some suggestions for topics to cover in the speech are as follows:
  - The happy couple's unique personalities
  - The groom's amusing childhood stories
  - How the couple first met
  - Compliments to the bridesmaids
  - Compliments to the bride's family
  - Compliments to the groom's family
  - The honeymoon
  - Their children/future children
  - Thanking the groom on behalf of the bridesmaids
  - The toast/finale.

Best man's duties

- Organize stag night
- Arrange suit fittings
- Look after groom on wedding day
- Responsible for buttonholes
- Keeper of the wedding ring
- Be in charge of gratuities
- Organize bride and groom's luggage
- Liaise between couple and venue management
- Speech.

Maid/matron of honour

The matron (married) or maid (single) of honour – or chief bridesmaid as she is often known – is chosen by the bride to become her most trusted adviser in the run up to the wedding.

- She is usually the bride's best and oldest friend who is able to give her honest advice and opinions throughout the preparations and take on some important tasks, for example organizing the hen night!
- Similarly to the best man, the maid of honour takes on a major role in the organization of the wedding, both before, during and after the event.
- She will generally help in making decisions that the groom is perhaps not particularly interested in, such as choosing stationery and helping the bride to write envelopes and place cards.
- Often she will help choose decorations and favours for the table and if there are any labours of love to be done, for example assembling favours, or designing and making menus, she may spend hours with the bride achieving the perfect look.
- One of the most fun periods in the lead up to a wedding are all the shopping trips that are required, from browsing through accessories to the most important of all, choosing the wedding dress! The maid of honour will be able to give the bride a truthful opinion of her choices, unhampered by the emotions of the bride's mother (who is likely to be consumed with pride and anticipation at every fitting).
- On the day of the wedding, she will come into her own, from keeping the bride serene and relaxed while they all get ready

to making sure she has eaten enough to sustain her until the reception (vital to eliminate any fainting, or nausea at the ceremony!).

- She will also manage the other bridesmaids, check the bride has her bag of essentials needed for the day and help her with her veil and train at the ceremony.
- The maid of honour usually: witnesses the signing of the marriage certificate, is included in the receiving line (if there is one) at the reception, is responsible for adding the finishing touches to the bridal suite, and ensures that the bride has everything she needs for the honeymoon, if the newlyweds are leaving the same night.
- She should also make sure that any hired or borrowed items are returned after the wedding.

Maid/matron of honour's duties

- Help bride to choose dress, stationery etc.
- Look after bride on wedding day
- Manage other bridesmaids
- Witness signing of register
- Check bride has everything she needs for honeymoon
- Return any hired/borrowed items.

Bridesmaids/pageboys

The tradition of bridesmaids dates back to pagan times, when it was thought that evil spirits would attend wedding ceremonies to bestow bad luck upon the happy couple. The idea was that by surrounding the bride with look-alike women, this would confuse the evil spirits and they would leave without casting a curse.

Nowadays the role of a bridesmaid is more of an assistant, than a decoy! Their role in both the planning and on the day is to help the event run perfectly. You may want to offer both girl and boy relatives and friends from both sides of the family the privilege of supporting the bride on her big day, but always be mindful that the costs can escalate considerably, with a large number of attendants to clothe and accessorize!

Bridesmaids'/pageboys' duties

- Look enchanting for the photographs
- Carry flowers or be a ring bearer.

Mother of the bride

Traditionally mothers have always played a major role in the planning of their daughter's wedding. However, their role seems to have become less significant in the planning stages nowadays, as couples either prefer to go it alone and manage the preparations themselves, or incorporate the services of a professional Wedding Planner to help organize the event. Statistics show that marriages are taking place later in a couple's life than was once the case. Today's bride is less likely to be living at home at the time of her marriage and has usually established a career. Therefore the couple generally have the means to finance the wedding independently, and want to make all the decisions themselves.

Mother of the bride's duties

- The mother of the bride often accompanies the bride at the meetings with her florist to share in the joy of choosing the displays for the day, and of course is generally with the bride when shopping for her wedding gown.
- On the wedding day, the bride's mother will travel with the bridesmaids to the church/ceremony and be the last guest to take her seat, escorted by one of the ushers.
- At the reception, she is able to relax and enjoy the day and should there be a receiving line, she should be at the head, acting as the hostess.

Father of the bride

One of the most moving moments of the wedding day is the part of the ceremony when the bride's father gives his daughter away. This special gesture symbolizes his blessing on the marriage and in particular his acceptance of his daughter's chosen husband.

Father of the bride's duties

- The father of the bride is usually involved in making any travel arrangements for relatives arriving before the day of the wedding and may act as chauffeur to his daughter and her mother on several of her shopping trips.
- He will be preparing his speech in the months leading up to the big day itself and supporting his family through this emotional time.
- On the wedding day itself, his role is to support his daughter and wife, give the bride away to the groom during the ceremony and to give a speech later at the reception.

Speeches

The groom, best man and father of the bride all have the unenviable task of entertaining guests with their wit, humour and heartfelt emotions, as well as dealing with the often daunting prospect of standing up and addressing hundreds of family members and friends in a manner that they are often not accustomed to.

Although most men choose to write their own speeches, given the choice they would be more than happy to receive help from a professional, who could give tips on presentation, relaxation techniques and witty good humour. There are many companies which specialize in providing speeches for every member of the bridal party (see bridal magazines and the internet).

Some speeches have become much more inventive in recent years. For example, there have been 'This is Your Life' style speeches made using the technology of an overhead projector to present images of the couple throughout their life. A tabloid editor once requested that a Planner print newspapers to be given to the guests, which were filled with sensational headlines and humorous photos, giving the best man a fabulous spring board for his speech. Another comic situation created by a best man was to give all the guests a 'Best Man Bingo Card' with certain words on it which, when mentioned in the speech, had to be crossed off. The first to cross off all the words won a bottle of champagne.

The bride does not usually make a speech, but occasionally the emotion and joy of the day take over and some brides are desperate to join in the fun and to voice their feelings at that moment. This is always received with great enthusiasm from the guests.

Coping with nerves

As performing a speech can be extremely nerve-wracking, some couples decide to have the speeches at the start of the wedding breakfast; this way, once the formalities are over, the best man, father of the bride and the groom can relax and enjoy their meal, without resorting to large quantities of alcohol for Dutch courage. Equally, the reverse can happen of course – that they are unable to eat or drink anything due to the nausea caused by their impending performances!

Order of speeches – who thanks who?

Traditionally there are three speeches.

1 The father of the bride is first and welcomes the groom's parents into the family.
2 Next is the groom who thanks his parents and parents-in-law and the bridesmaids.
3 Finally the best man speaks and closes the speeches with a toast to the bride and groom.

Who pays for what?

Thankfully for the bride's father, times have changed since he was liable to pay for the whole event! Customarily, financial responsibility was as follows:

The bride's parents	The bride's dress, bridesmaid's outfits, stationery, flowers, the reception, photography, wedding cards and cake
The groom	His outfit, rings, church costs, attendants' gifts, bridesmaids' bouquets, ushers' buttonholes and honeymoon.

Although this has been the traditional way the finances have been divided, it is increasingly common for the couple to pay for the entire day themselves with perhaps contributions from both sides of the family put towards various aspects of the wedding costs. Both sets of parents will usually make a monetary donation to ease the burden of the final account for the couple.

Seating plans

Organising a seating plan is notoriously difficult and can be one of the most time-consuming jobs to complete. You may even have to juggle seating arrangements around right up to the last minute and even on the day itself, so be prepared to be flexible and ensure you have made a drawn plan of the room and table layout to help you.

The top table includes key members of the bridal party as follows with the bride traditionally sitting on the left of the groom:

chief bridesmaid, groom's father, bride's mother, groom, bride, bride's father, groom's mother and best man.

However, in some cases the modern family unit (including stepmothers, half-brothers etc.) makes it difficult to include everyone on the top table. It is therefore usual that the stepparents are not part of the bridal party, but instead they would be seated, as honoured guests, on a table that is nearest to the top table.

With regard to invited couples, it is a good idea to place them on the same table, although they do not necessarily have to sit next to each other. If you have any guests who you know would not get on with each other, you would be well advised to separate them. Small children should preferably be seated with their parents, or perhaps on a special children's table, either in the same room or – if you have the space – they could be supervized and entertained elsewhere (see 'Entertaining the children' in Chapter 11).

Top tip

I often advise couples to break with tradition and have an oval or round table as the top table, which allows for everyone to socialize better and does not leave anyone with the feeling of exclusion (which oftens happens when seated on trestle tables with individuals on each end). This would also help in situations with stepparents, as larger tables could accommodate all members of the family and the top table would not feel so exposed and on show.

Receiving line

The practice of having a receiving line at the reception – to lead guests into the wedding breakfast – is quite useful, allowing the bridal party to greet each individual guest in turn, particularly as there may not have been time to meet everyone during the ceremony or reception. Do bear in mind however, that if you have a large guest list, there will be a considerable queue; keep acknowledgements to a brief 'hello' and do not enter into any lengthy conversations, as you will create a frustrated line of well-wishers! During a formal reception, you may choose to employ a Master of Ceremonies who will announce each of your guests; this practice is becoming less popular, as increasingly couples choose to have a more informal approach to the day.

Top tip

If you do decide to have a 'line up', it is always a good idea to serve your waiting guests with a drink and canapés, so that they are kept occupied while queuing. Keep it moving; you will hopefully have time to have a longer chat throughout the evening. At this point, everyone is anxious to sit down and most guests are getting hungry, so do not delay too long! You could perhaps arrange for a magician to go along the line performing 'slight-of-hand' tricks, which will keep everyone entranced and amused while they wait.

Stag and hen parties

Traditionally, the best man and maid of honour are in charge of organizing the pre-nuptial festivities. Sensibly, modern grooms are becoming more responsible and realize that their enjoyment of the day (and that of their bride) could be seriously impaired if they are suffering as a result of being led astray by their best man the night before the wedding. The majority of grooms opt for a celebration a couple of weeks before the big day, allowing them plenty of time to recover! The bride also tends to gather her friends during a day or weekend of fun, some weeks before the wedding. The options open to both of them today have moved on considerably from the days of a simple evening get-together at the local pub.

The groom and his stags could choose from a number of options. These include physical activities such as paint-balling, golf, sailing, quad biking, or perhaps a visit to the races.

The girls may choose to spend a weekend away in a European city, for example Paris or Amsterdam, or even a shopping trip to New York! Nearer home they may opt for a spa or country house hotel for a few days of pampering, which is becoming increasingly popular. However, there is usually a considerable cost involved in these options; some brides prefer to have a night out in a restaurant or nightclub for a larger number of friends and reserve the trips away for closer family and friends, as it may be prohibitive to ask everyone to contribute.

Here are some other wonderful ideas for hen nights:

- Professional makeover and photo session; make-up and hair stylists will transform your looks and a professional photographer will capture the 'new you' on celluloid.
- Stay in a rural cottage for the night and enrol in a local jewellery course, making beaded necklaces, earrings and gorgeous goodies.
- Employ a professional chef to visit your house and cook for you and your friends; if Jamie Oliver is not free, try contacting a good local restaurateur and enquiring about his fee.
- Hire a cabin or two aboard a train and wake up in the Highlands to the sound of piped music and bubbling porridge for breakfast.
- Book a long boat on one of England's many canal routes, stopping at rural pubs along the way.

- Why not record your own version of your favourite pop song in a professional studio and take home a CD to play to your heart's content?
- Book a cocktail specialist such as Cocktail Heaven to come to your home or a venue to entertain Tom Cruise style! They will supply barmen to teach you how to mix your favourite cocktails and keep you enthralled – perfect for fans of the film *Cocktail* and all the fun of the 'flair'!
- Arrange a Murder Mystery night! Give everyone a part and instructions on how to dress, and you will have a fantastic night to remember! There are numerous games on the market to choose from, depending on the style of evening you would like to create.
- A fan of James Bond? Well, how about being a spy for a day? Experience days are extremely popular and provide fun and frolics for hen parties with a difference! Learn some of the essential skills required to conduct a secret agent operation! Covert cameras, bugs, listening devices and lock-picking gadgets are all used in the preparation for your mission. Try your skill at axe throwing and test your nerve and concentration with a bomb deactivation challenge. You could also receive some expert instruction on unarmed combat techniques (see the Taking it further section).
- You could even combine your hen party with your partner's stag day and recreate a hostage rescue or a diamond heist! Working together as a team using new skills learnt to conduct a plan, an ex-SAS Commander will guide you through the intelligence to complete the mission with the finale played out in a helicopter trip – to either rescue the victim or steal the precious jewels!

02 the planning

In this chapter you will learn:

- **how to plan your day**
- **the average costs involved and setting a budget**
- **the role of the wedding planner**
- **the importance of scheduling and time-frames**
- **how to source information**
- **how to book suppliers**
- **the importance of insurance**
- **how to deal with stress.**

How? When? Where? How much?

One of the most important decisions in the initial stages of planning your wedding is how much you would like to spend and – more importantly – are able to spend. It is crucial that you have a clear idea of the amount of funds, as it is very easy to be persuaded to part with a great deal of your hard-earned cash along the way and you do not want to start married life with a large debt to repay!

Recent wedding surveys have shown that over 50 per cent of couples contribute the bulk of the money; if you do intend to fund the whole wedding yourselves, it is useful to open a dedicated wedding account and create a financial spreadsheet to help you stick to your budget. If a computerized account is not suitable for your situation, at least buy a ledger book where you will be able to enter by hand all the relevant expenses and keep a close eye on your expenditure.

It is at this point that you should have a discussion with both sets of parents to find out whether they would like/are able to make an offer of financial help and if there is any specific aspect of the wedding they would prefer to contribute towards.

AVERAGE COSTS (2007)

Engagement ring	£1200
Bride's wedding ring	£360
Groom's wedding ring	£316
Bride's dress	£860
Shoes	£89
Veil and headdress	£96
Jewellery	£118
Attendants' outfits	£529
Bride's going away outfit	£109
Special lingerie	£75
Cosmetics	£88
Photography	£838
Professional video	£539
Flowers	£458
Transport	£380
Stationery	£239
Ceremony fees	£347
Attendants' gifts	£177

Catering and food	£3068
Drink	£946
Cake	£243
Hire of venue	£2291
Entertainment	£598
First night hotel	£235
Honeymoon	£2938
TOTAL	£17,137

Weddings on a budget

If finances are limited, it does not mean that the wedding will be any less fabulous. In fact, some of the best weddings are those where budgets have been tight and therefore a great deal more thought has gone into every detail, to make it particularly special; this often produces very personal, unique touches.

A wedding is primarily about the people with whom you choose to share the celebration, rather than the potential scale and grandeur – which can sometimes overshadow the true meaning of the day. As much as a couple may yearn for the spectacular dream wedding, if funds are limited it forces you to really think about the most important aspects of your particular wedding day, and how to maximize the impact!

Wedding Planners

I started my own wedding consultancy business over 15 years ago at a time when it was relatively unusual to use a professional to organize a wedding; that role was traditionally taken by the mother of the bride who would relish the task of helping and guiding her daughter through every aspect of the day. Today there are hundreds of Wedding Planners in the UK, providing varied services to couples the length and breadth of the country.

- The US has known the advantage of employing a professional Wedding Planner for many years and since the early 1990s the industry has successfully grown in the UK. This growth is primarily due to the fact that although today's modern couple tend to want to finance the wedding themselves and to take the lead in making the decisions, they are nevertheless generally in full-time employment and lack the amount of time or knowledge required to embark on such a huge event; they are simply unable or unwilling to spend their free time at weekends and evenings visiting venues and sourcing suppliers.

- A Planner is employed to act independently, sourcing the best possible solutions to each and every aspect of the wedding, researching new suppliers and products, obtaining discounts on behalf of their clients and using their first-hand knowledge to provide the couple with a pleasurable experience in the run up to the wedding day, free from any concern or doubt.
- A proficient Wedding Planner will have built up a comprehensive network of contacts and will have proven themselves to be reliable, professional individuals. A couple choosing the services of a Wedding Planner will hope that their requests will be noted and acted upon efficiently, they will be provided with expert advice and guidance and offered complete reassurance and the guarantee that their very special day is in safe hands!
- Generally a Planner develops an extremely close bond with clients throughout the weeks and months leading up to their wedding, and gains their clients' trust in their judgement to achieve the ultimate service, with the least amount of stress or anxiety.
- This is heightened on the day itself when a Planner comes into their own, by eliminating any possibility of an anxious moment for whatever reason, as she/he is there to ensure the day runs smoothly: managing deliveries, checking schedules and being the couple's fairy godmother, granting that every wish and minute detail of the day is fulfilled to perfection!
- The cost of a Wedding Planner's services vary and couples should make enquiries to several companies, before making a final decision (which is usually based on personality, rather than cost alone). Companies often have a 'package' cost (organizing a range of services with varying fees) or alternatively will work on a commission basis, with the fee dependent on the final account and expenditure. It is generally considered that their fees are good value as they are able to negotiate significant discounts and favourable rates with suppliers (as they provide them with repeat business). Their clients receive the reassurance of quality services from suppliers who are keen to work for the Planners again and who therefore will act in a conscientious, professional manner.

Choosing the day

There are a number of superstitions concerning the day on which you are married. For example, some think that it is best to avoid the thirteenth in any month! One famous rhyme advises:

Monday for wealth,
Tuesday for health,
Wednesday the best of all,
Thursday for crosses,
Friday for losses and
Saturday for no luck at all!

Luckily the sentiment of this rhyme does not seem to have influenced the choice of the majority, as Saturday is generally the most popular day for weddings, with Friday as a second choice if the venue is fully booked. Sunday and weekday weddings are usually offered by venues at a discounted rate. This would allow room for negotiation, however they are rarely a popular choice as friends and family are less likely to want to celebrate late into the night when they have to work the following day!

When deciding on the actual date, you need firstly to check with key members of your family and friends that they are available. Then it always advisable to consider any major sporting events that may be scheduled for the same day as your wedding. Otherwise you may have frustrated guests waiting for vital scores, or some strays disappearing halfway through the day to watch an important match!

Which season?

An English summer wedding – what could be more beautiful? However, it is advisable to err on the side of caution and assume that sunshine may not be entirely guaranteed and so make provision for inclement weather. You must also take into consideration that the summer months between May and September are the most sought after for weddings and bookings should be made as far in advance as possible to avoid disappointment.

A spring wedding, evoking images of an abundance of scented daffodils, may be somewhat easier when it comes to a venue's availability, as is autumn with its warm earthy tones. Winter weddings, with romantic thoughts of guests gathered around roaring log fires are increasingly popular as there are no false hopes about the weather. However, venues with character and charm and a welcoming interior are sought-after in this season. If you choose to get married nearer Christmas, check the church calendar before making any assumptions as there are certain dates on which marriages cannot take place, and some churches will have restrictions on flower displays and hymns.

What time of day?

When you are deciding at what time to schedule the ceremony, bear in mind the style of day that you would like. For example, if you have invited all your guests to the ceremony and would like them to join you for the entire day, the following timetable is the simplest option to organize as it does not leave anyone with time on their hands between the ceremony and an evening function.

Church service	1 hour
Photographs	30 minutes
Travel to venue	30 minutes
Reception	1–1½ hours
Wedding Breakfast	2 hours

Following this timetable, if the church service started at 2p.m., the Wedding Breakfast would finish at 7.30p.m., perfect timing to start the evening entertainment/dancing.

However, if you wish to have an earlier, morning ceremony, followed by lunch for immediate family and friends, with more guests invited for an evening celebration, there will be a gap in the day after the meal. Therefore you should ensure that your guests are catered for, either with entertainment (especially if there are any children involved) or with facilities available for them to relax and enjoy their day, perhaps in the lounge of a hotel, and refreshments.

Top tip

Always work out the timing well in advance and discuss the schedule with your minister/registrar, photographer, transport supervisor and the management at the venue, so everyone is aware of the timescale they are working towards.

The itinerary

One of the most valuable exercises in the planning stage is to initiate and finalize the itinerary. This schedule of your wedding day will be your Bible and copies should be given to all suppliers and key personnel, so that the day runs as smoothly as possible. It should include a detailed list of timings for everyone involved in the wedding. Start with the earliest delivery, what time your make-up artist is arriving, the collection of the buttonholes, through to the schedule at the venue and who is responsible for each duty, and finally including any transport booked to take you or guests home at the end of the evening. By making this timed itinerary as detailed as possible, it will enable all the key players to know what they and their associates should be doing at any point in the day, and will help to get things back on track if there are any delays or mishaps along the way.

Year planner

Most couples start preparing for their wedding approximately a year in advance, which allows for a greater choice of venues, as well as other suppliers who will become booked up very quickly. The following full year planner will guide you through the 12 months leading up to the wedding.

Things to do now

- Tell friends and relatives that you are engaged
- Place an announcement in the newspaper
- Open a wedding bank account
- Organize wedding insurance
- Decide on a budget and agree who is paying for what
- Choose your best man, usher and bridesmaids

12–6 months before

- Agree a date for a church or civil ceremony
- Check that principal friends and family members are available
- Search for and book the venue
- Consider employing the services of a Wedding Planner
- Book the church and pay any deposits due to secure the date
- Liaise between the church/registrar and venue to confirm both at the same time

- Start looking for your florist, photographer, transport, caterers, cake maker
- If you need a marquee, make appointments to discuss the services of several companies
- Decide on your stationery and place order – send out 'save the date' cards if required
- Plan and book your honeymoon
- Decide on the style of entertainment: band, disco etc. and confirm booking
- Draw up a draft guest list so that you have a rough idea of numbers
- Start looking at wedding dress and bridesmaid styles and designs in magazines and arrange shopping days to try on different styles
- Decide on the wedding gown and bridesmaids' outfits
- Begin a beauty/fitness regime

6–4 months before

- Choose your gift list company
- Visit your minister/priest to discuss the ceremony, music, readings, musicians etc.
- Organize suits for the groom, best man and ushers, if required
- If you have made a 'no children' rule at the wedding, make this perfectly clear so parents are able to make arrangements
- Book additional services for the day, such as children's entertainer
- Check proofs for stationery and give final approval
- Choose and purchase wedding rings
- Order your wedding cake
- Buy wedding lingerie
- Choose or start making your favours or gifts for guests
- Reserve any necessary accommodation for guests

4–2 months before

- Organize any inoculations for the honeymoon, finalize plans, check passports are up to date, book travel insurance
- Send out invitations, including gift list information and any travel details
- Book trial hair and make-up sessions to discuss options – make sure you have any accessories, such as tiaras or headdresses with you, so that you can see the final look

- Indulge in some pampering treatments
- Buy going away outfit – if required
- Finalize all readings, music etc. with the church, so that Order of Service sheets can be approved and printed
- Arrange a meeting with florist to finalize details
- Book a meeting with photographer at venue, so that they can become familiar with the surroundings and choose ideal locations for the best shots
- Book any menu tasting with the caterer
- Finalize groom's outfits and those of ushers/best man
- Finalize bridesmaids' outfits, allowing for growth of young children over the coming months
- Write your personalized wedding vows if necessary
- Schedule rehearsal time and rehearsal dinner
- Book first night hotel if necessary

2–1 months before

- Draw up final list of guests from RSVPs
- Start working on the seating plan
- Write thank you notes as and when gifts arrive
- Book your final hair appointment
- Finalize transport and check any travel restrictions for the wedding day
- Organize hen and stag parties for at least one week before the wedding
- Notify bank, doctor etc. if you are changing your name
- Decide on the list of shots required and send to photographer
- Organize traveller's cheques/foreign currency for honeymoon, if necessary

1 month before

- Contact all suppliers and double-check arrangements and timings
- Chase up outstanding RSVPs
- Compile musical selection for the band/disco
- Book bride's final dress fitting

2 weeks before

- Confirm final numbers with your caterer and discuss any specific dietary needs

- Bride to try on complete outfit with accessories, lingerie etc. so that there is time to make any final changes
- Have your hen and stag nights and any work drinks during this week

1 week before

- Check on the weather forecast for the day and make any provisions, for example umbrellas, sunshades, heating
- Arrange for the cake to be delivered to the venue
- Wear in your wedding shoes at home
- Confirm final details with photographer, caterer, florist, transport, entertainment and all suppliers
- Contact bridal party to confirm that everyone is clear about their own duties

Day before

- Organize for the honeymoon luggage to be sent to your first night hotel if necessary
- Bride to pamper herself, with a manicure, pedicure, massage and a relaxation session – yoga is a wonderful discipline to use if you are familiar with the positions and breathing techniques

On the day (bride)

- Have a long soak in a bubble bath, or an invigorating shower before everyone starts arriving to help you
- Make sure you have enough to eat before you leave, so that you are not feeling faint!
- Let your bridesmaids fuss over you and help with the little ones, while you concentrate on yourself

On the day (groom)

- Relax! Perhaps meet friends for a pre-wedding lunch, but try to stay calm and not worry about the rest of the day. Everything is out of your hands now, so try to enjoy it.

These duties should be done by others on the day/after the day

- Make sure the best man has the rings
- Make sure the best man has collected the buttonholes and corsages for the groom's side of the wedding, if the florist has delivered all the flowers to the bride's house

- Return hired items to relevant suppliers
- Pack and take home wedding presents
- Send wedding cake to those unable to attend

Wedding shows

Why spend weeks and months requesting supplier's brochures, visiting designers' showrooms, trawling the internet and sitting for hours on the phone, when you can spend one day in a relaxed and focused environment at a wedding show, where you may be able to find everything you need? These shows serve couples and their friends and family with hundreds of ideas, and are a fantastic source of inspiration. Many brides will travel a great distance to get to one of the leading shows around the country, as they know that they will come away at the end of the day with a goody bag packed full of business cards, brochures and samples of work from some of the top suppliers in the wedding industry. It is a wonderful start to the preparations as you will be able to have first-hand experience of an array of products and services – all under the one roof – which, if suitable, will save you a great deal of time and effort. The shows are well organized and professionally run, with exciting catwalk fashion shows showcasing many of the top designers, which are always a pleasure to watch. Even if some of the couture dresses are beyond your budget, it often inspires you to decide what outfits you absolutely love and which ones might suit your style and theme for the day. By visiting the stands, you should be able to try on sample gowns, which is great fun and gives you the chance to see for the first time how you might want to look on the day. The exhibitors will be keen for your business and therefore will be active in promoting their services. If you have allowed the day to browse and peruse the stands, it will give you a chance to meet and chat with them; firstly this is a perfect way of finding out if they are offering the type of service you want and secondly if they are friendly, professional people who instil the confidence that they will provide a good, thorough service. Often wedding cake suppliers will not only have designs of their cakes for you to view, but will offer sample pieces of cake for tasting, which is very useful and saves a visit to their shop later on. Musicians generally play in the foyer, or take space of their own on a stand, and being able to hear their performance first-hand is a great advantage and allows you to enjoy their music and imagine them playing at your own wedding! There will even be wedding cars and limousines there for you to sit inside and judge whether there is sufficient room for the bride, her gown and the groom as well!

The National Wedding Show – England

The leading wedding shows are organized by the National Wedding Show (www.nationalweddingshow.co.uk) twice a year. The first two shows are held in Olympia, London and the NEC, Birmingham in February, and then again in September at Earls Court, London and the NEC, Birmingham. The four shows a year are renowned for introducing a vast number of companies to couples who may not have the opportunity of meeting new, innovative suppliers in person; with them all being under the one roof, it puts the fun back into the planning stages, saves the legwork and allows you to relax and enjoy all the benefits of such an established show. With regular features such as free makeovers, a champagne bar and an Inspiration Zone – where you can get expert advice – it has something for everyone!

The Designer Wedding Show – London

The Designer Wedding Show (www.designerweddingshow.co.uk) in Battersea Park in February each year features the elite of the wedding world, with hand-picked designers and suppliers to create your dream day. This chic wedding event is staged in a stylish venue in the middle of leafy Battersea and the finest companies and designers are selected for their delectable detail and passion for quality and style.

The Scottish Wedding Show – Glasgow and Edinburgh

The Scottish Wedding Show (www.scottishweddingshow.co.uk) held in Glasgow attracts nearly 9000 brides (there are 28,000 weddings held in Scotland every year). The main shows in February and September. Each has over 200 exhibitors, offering services from free make-up sessions, to honeymoons, competitions to win your dream wedding, wine tasting and spectacular fashions on the catwalk, not forgetting those handsome Scotsmen in their traditional kilts!

The Asian Wedding Exhibition – London

The Asian Wedding Exhibition (www.aweuk.com) at Alexandra Palace in London every February has established itself as the leading show for Asian brides and their families and has a wealth of exhibitors to cater for all your needs.

Local regional wedding shows

Most town and cities around the UK will host a wedding show at some time throughout the year, usually in the summer or in February (around Valentine's Day). Keep an eye out in your local newspapers, or magazines for advertisements, as these will generally take place in a hotel or venue suitable for a wedding reception and will allow you to see it set up for a wedding, with smaller businesses offering local wedding services that could be just what you are looking for!

Booking suppliers

The majority of wedding suppliers offer professional, good quality products and services. However, unfortunately – as in any industry – there is a minority which give bad press to the rest by providing a less than adequate service.

Often a brochure or photograph is requested – for example, a horse and carriage service – and you would hope that if it is suitable for your needs, all you need to do is book it on the phone. Please do not take this risk, unless you have been recommended to use the company by a close and trusted friend. On more than one occasion, couples have been sent photographs of a well-groomed horse pulling a stunningly beautiful carriage; however, having made an appointment to view the vehicle, they were horrified to find a broken, torn, dirty carriage, hooked to an out-of-condition old nag!

Top tip

It is vital that you find the time to inspect the condition of any provisionally booked trannsport before making your final decision; you do not want to be disappointed on the day when the car of your dreams turns into a rusty old banger arriving on the morning of your wedding day! If you have heard about a particular band or discotheque that you are interested in, make an appointment to attend a function at which they are playing, perhaps in a local hotel or private venue, and discreetly watch and listen to them play, so that you know first-hand if they are suitable for your needs. Keep in touch with suppliers in the lead up to the wedding and confirm details well in advance.

Tips and advice are given later in the book for each supplier and the dos and don'ts of booking both individuals and companies.

Checking and double-checking

One of the most crucial pieces of advice is DO NOT MAKE ASSUMPTIONS! Do not think that by confirming your bookings 12–6 months in advance that all will be well, you do not need to contact your suppliers again and that they will just turn up on the day and provide the service you have discussed. Thankfully, in most cases, the majority will of course act professionally and conscientiously, providing exactly what you have asked for in a prompt and efficient manner. However, it is very important to bear in mind that these businesses are dealing with many more events than your wedding alone and for your own peace of mind, if nothing else, it is advisable to contact them periodically in the run up to the wedding to discuss your booking. Keep them updated with any changes, amendments or new additions to your schedule and finally, a few days before the day, give them a call just to check and double-check that all is well. This one simple phone call will ease your mind and iron out any last minute queries – sadly it has been proven time and time again that it is often the one element of the preparations that has not been thoroughly checked that causes problems, resulting in panic and disappointment so near to your big day, which could so easily have been avoided!

Insurance

Before you send off any deposits, it is advisable to consider taking out a specialist wedding insurance policy, to cover any unforeseen events prior to the day, or on the actual day itself. The minimal cost involved in comparison to the total amount of a wedding is really worth serious consideration, as it may save a great deal of money in the long run, and alleviate some of the anxiety should things not turn out exactly the way you had planned! A wedding insurance policy will cover such items as: cancellation due to illness or bereavement; public liability insurance; if a guest is injured in an accident at the venue; also any loss or damage of wedding presents, as well as covering any damage to the bridal attire, which could be very useful, for instance if any wine is spilt on the day.

Most deposits would be refunded through the policy and if for example, the photographer does not turn up, the insurance would pay for a retake of the photographs.

Most insurance companies would cover the following aspects of a wedding. This is an example of a standard policy; for full details you will need to contact the insurance companies direct.

- **Cancellation and expenses**
  If you have to cancel or unexpectedly curtail your wedding.
- **Supplier deposits**
  Cover your non-refundable deposits, in the event of financial failure of the suppliers or if entertainers fail to appear.
- **Your wedding attire**
  For loss, or damage while in your possession and occurring prior to wedding commencement or financial failure of suppliers.
- **Photographs and video**
  For all expenses in the retaking of the official photographs or video, loss or damage, faulty materials or non-appearance of the photographer or video cameraman.
- **Presents**
  For loss or damage within 24 hours before and after the wedding.
- **Rings**
  For loss or damage occurring within seven days of the wedding.
- **Cake**
  Loss or damage within 24 hours before the wedding.
- **Personal accident**
  For accidental bodily injury during the period of insurance.
- **Wedding cars and transport**
  Failure of transport due to breakdown, accident or non-appearance when a contract is in force.
- **Flowers**
  Loss or damage up to seven days prior to the wedding day.
- **Legal expenses**
  Legal costs and expenses incurred by the bride and groom arising from the wedding or reception having to be cancelled.
- **Public liability**
  Legal liability to a third party for the damages and costs arising from an incident at your wedding service, reception or evening function.

- **Honeymoon luggage**
  Loss or damage on the day of the reception.
- **Documents/Passports**
  Expenses incurred due to loss or damage of wedding documents or passports within seven days of departure or whilst abroad.
- **Luggage/Property**
  For loss or damage to personal property for the duration of the honeymoon.
- **Delayed travel**
  Compensation or costs incurred following unexpected and unavoidable delayed travel.
- **Professional counselling**
  Cover for the cost of guidance if your wedding should fail to take place.

Health and fitness

Every couple would hope to feel that they are at the peak of their fitness on their wedding day, so that they are able to enjoy every moment of what is usually an extremely long and tiring day. It is therefore sensible to think about your general well-being at the start of the preparations, so that you allow sufficient time to gain the benefits of a health and fitness programme, no matter how strict or relaxed the regime.

You may want to join a gym, to encourage regular exercise, start a skin and hair care programme, or simply go for a jog in the park on a Sunday afternoon! Whatever you choose, you will definitely reap the rewards come your wedding day.

Why not take advantage of a free hair trial offered by department stores for brides and their mothers or friends? This is a great way to glean tips and advice from experts, which you will be able to use on the day. There are often special offers available and products can be tried before you have to purchase them.

Bridal magazines

Bridal magazines are a fantastic source of inspiration in the run up to your wedding day and are packed full of wonderful hairstyles, make-up and outfits suitable for the whole bridal party! They are a very pleasurable way of gleaning inspirational ideas and are generally the first purchase an engaged bride-to-be will make. Perfect for expert knowledge, up-to-date ideas and tips, they have articles on every detail of the day, including: flower arrangements, table settings, fashion trends, venue news and a comprehensive classified section offering a huge variety of suppliers. The first time you open a magazine and are confronted with page after glossy page of stunning, exquisite bridal gowns, wedding cakes decorated with soft pastel coloured icing, fabulous bouquets of gorgeous flowers and reams of new ideas and suggestions for the perfect day, your heart will be filled with anticipation and excitement for your own plans and expectations.

Stress busters

Laughter is the best form of defence, so they say, and during the stressful time of organizing a wedding, the ability to find the funny side of a situation is invaluable.

There will be many occasions when emotions will get the better of you and your relatives and if you are able to make light of the matter, it will save any arguments or cross words uttered in the heat of the moment, which later you may regret.

If you find that relatives are becoming a little too involved with each and every aspect of your wedding day, and perhaps you feel that the reins are being taken away from you, stop and consider for a moment. Remember, this is *your* wedding and you should have exactly what *you* want and not have to accept the ideas and plans of your well-meaning family, just because you want an easy life. Try to be as diplomatic as possible, but ensure that you make your own feelings very clear and insist on the final decision being yours. If it all gets too much, why don't you both escape the anxiety and tension at home and arrange a weekend away, making a pact not to discuss the wedding at all (if at all possible); just use the time to relax, unwind and recharge your batteries before returning to rejoin the madness in the run up to the big day.

the formalities

In this chapter you will learn:

- **about the legal requirements – licences etc.**
- **the Church of England/ Catholic requirements**
- **suggestions for readings**
- **about civil partnerships**
- **about humanist blessings**
- **about second marriages**
- **how to marry abroad**
- **about marrying a foreign national**
- **information on Asian weddings.**

Civil or church ceremony?

Church of England

The Church of England stipulates that the wedding service must take place between 8a.m. and 6p.m. and couples have the right to be married in the parish church of the town where they are resident, or in the church where one or other of the couple are on the church's electoral roll. If you are not sure of your local parish church, the Church of England website (www.cofe.anglican.org) has a 'search by postcode' service, which is quick and simple to use. You do not have to be regularly attending church to get married in the Church of England, or have to have been baptized, as long as you choose to marry in your local parish church. Once you have met your parish minister and checked dates, notice is given by either party to the Superintendent Registrar in the district where one of you lives.

Publication of the Banns

As a couple, you may be expected to meet the minister several times before the publication of the Banns so he/she is satisfied that you understand the full implications of the commitment of marriage. What publication of the Banns means in practice is the public announcement by the minister during a normal church service that two people wish to marry, and an invitation to the congregation to declare any unlawful reason why they should not marry. An application for the publication of the Banns should be made to the church of the parish in which each one of you lives, for which you will have to pay a small fee. A certificate stating that the Banns have been published will be issued by the church that will not be holding the ceremony. This certificate needs to be produced to the officiating minister before the ceremony can go ahead. On the three Sundays prior to the wedding, the Banns are read out in the parish church (or churches) of the couple. Banns are effective for three months after publication. If the couple live in different parishes, the Banns need to be published in both parishes. But don't forget – if the marriage does not take place within three months of the publication of the Banns then they will have to be published again.

Choosing a church outside of your local parish

If you are listed on the church's electoral role, you will be able to marry in a parish other than your local parish church, as long as it is the church that you both usually attend. You will need to plan ahead to do this and have a minister with an open mind. If you need to become enlisted on the electoral role of a church in another parish, at least one of you must regularly attend that church for a minimum period of six months and that person must be a baptized member of the Church of England. Note: The church electoral roll is different to the local register of electors. So, if you wish to get married in a church which is not your own, then contact the minister of that church well in advance of the date on which you wish to be married and he will be able to advise you.

Common Licence

A marriage between two foreigners or between a foreigner and a British subject should be by licence. It is recommended that the Common Licence is used for people who are only living temporarily in the parish in which they wish the marriage to take place. If a British couple who are no longer resident in England or Wales wish to marry, then a Common Licence should be applied for and is required if one party – although normally living in England – does not have British nationality. This also applies in cases where one party – although having British nationality – is not normally resident in England. It is a legal requirement that at least one of the couple must be resident at a *bona fide* address within the parish where the marriage is to take place for a minimum of 15 consecutive days immediately prior to the issuing of the licence, which is then valid for three months. The Diocesan Bishop authorizes the licence, and application is usually made to the Bishop's Surrogate for Marriage Licences for that area (the minister at the church may be the Surrogate but if not, he would know who should be contacted).

Although it is not thought that moving to an address in a parish for the required number of days – for example, to a local hotel – for the sole reason of qualifying to marry there should be grounds for a refusal to issue a Common Licence, it should be remembered that the decision to issue one is discretionary. Also, legally, it is not considered sufficient to leave a suitcase at an address in the parish or to assume residency by some other bogus means, and that it is actually a criminal offence to give false information when applying for a licence. If the licence is granted, the vicar should not refuse to solemnize the marriage.

To be married by Common Licence:

- At least one of you must have been baptized.
- The ceremony must take place within three months of the licence being listed.
- There must be a good reason for requesting a Common Licence, for example, one party living abroad that prevents Banns from being read.

Special Licence

Marriage by Special Licence is unusual and it must be approved by the Archbishop of Canterbury at the Faculty Office. If a couple wish to marry in a parish where neither party is resident or on the electoral roll, or they are unable to satisfy the 15-day minimum residence requirement necessary for a Common Licence, a Special Licence will need to be granted. Although there is no minimum residence requirement, it is usually only granted in exceptional (special or emergency) circumstances. An application will not be considered unless the minister at the church in question is prepared to take both the marriage service and to support the licence application. Once granted, the licence is valid for three months.

Catholic church

If both parties are Catholic ...

If you are both Roman Catholic, your parishes will announce your forthcoming weddings during the three consecutive Sunday services preceding the wedding with the publication of Banns, although this practice tends to happen more in rural areas than in the city, where the practice has become less common. This allows any member of the congregation the opportunity to inform the priest of any objections they may have and is used to replace the well-known question during the ceremony: 'Does anyone know of any reason why this couple should not be joined together in Holy Matrimony?'

You will need to complete a number of forms to say that both of you agree with the church's view of marriage and that you are legally, spiritually and freely able to marry. However, if you decide to marry at a church other than your local church, you will need to seek special permission from the Roman Catholic authorities.

If one partner is not Catholic ...

In the case that one partner is not Catholic, the parish priest will have to consider whether to apply for a Dispensation to Marry. This is a permit issued by the Catholic Church giving permission for a Catholic to marry someone who is not and the priest will apply for this after speaking to both of you, to make sure that you are aware of the Catholic Church's attitudes towards marriage – that the Catholic partner understands the obligations they will undertake, and that you are both fully aware of the problems that can arise in mixed-faith marriages, such as the faith of any subsequent children.

It is important to note that a priest cannot refuse to give dispensation to marry if he is not happy about the motives of the couple; he has to ask his bishop to make the final decision. If only one partner is Roman Catholic, Banns are not published and the priest of the Roman Catholic partner will have to give permission for the marriage to take place either in a Roman Catholic Church or a non-Roman Catholic Church. You will need to prove to the Superintendent Registrar that the church is your normal place of worship, if the church where you wish to marry is in a different registration district. If you cannot do this, you will be required to give notice in the registration district in which the church is situated after having met the necessary residency requirement.

Your parish priest

You will need to make an appointment with your parish priest early on in the planning, to check availability of your chosen dates and to arrange your involvement in any marriage courses the parish may offer, known as 'pre-canna sessions'. These include issues such as:

- communication
- money
- coping with conflict
- sex
- in-laws and family issues
- children.

Preparation classes

Although it would probably be the parish priest who would run these meetings, laypeople will often attend to give advice. If you do not know your parish priest well, this is a way of improving your relationship with him and becoming familiar with the church where the wedding will take place. The wedding ceremony itself will be greatly enhanced by having someone perform the ceremony with whom you have formed a bond and hopefully a lasting friendship.

Father William Hebborn, of St Anselm's Parish, South London, says: 'Love isn't just a feeling, love is a decision. A feeling is like the weather; it is always changing and we have to acknowledge that despite those changes, you have taken the Covenant of Love, given your oath, your promise to your spouse that you will be with them in sickness, in health, ... till death do you part. Commitment is the life blood of marriage and communication, is crucial to the success of a partnership – exchange information, talk about your interests, share political views, but most importantly, share who you are, talk about how you feel, your needs. Consideration for each other's personal space and respecting the aspirations of your partner will strengthen your bond. Love is being able to set another person free. Sometimes we build up a protective barrier because we do not want to be hurt. Everyone needs to know that they are loved, unconditionally and that someone is there for you who knows and understands you for what and who you are.' He adds: 'At its best, love shows itself in moments of illumination, of grace that confirms your faith and the deep bond you have for each other – it is at this time that you realize you are truly loved.'

Bible readings

It is a personal choice which readings to have during the ceremony; however, your priest will be able to offer some suggestions to help you choose pieces that mean something special to you both. These are some of the more popular choices.

NT–5 I Corinthians 12:31–13:13

If I do not have love, I gain nothing.

If I speak in the tongues of men and of angels, but have not love, I am only a resounding gong or a clanging cymbal. If I have the gift of prophecy and can fathom all mysteries and all knowledge, and if I have a faith that can move mountains, but have not love, I am nothing. If I give all I possess to the poor and surrender my body to the flames, but have not love, I gain nothing.

Love is patient, love is kind. It does not envy, it does not boast, it is not proud. It is not rude, it is not self-seeking, it is not easily angered, it keeps no record of wrongs. Love does not delight in evil but rejoices with the truth. It always protects, always trusts, always hopes, always perseveres.

Love never fails. But where there are prophecies, they will cease; where there are tongues, they will be stilled; where there is knowledge, it will pass away. For we know in part and we prophesy in part, but when perfection comes, the imperfect disappears. When I was a child, I talked like a child, I thought like a child, I reasoned like a child. When I became a man, I put childish ways behind me. Now we see but a poor reflection as in a mirror; then we shall see face to face. Now I know in part; then I shall know fully, even as I am fully known.

And now these three remain: faith, hope and love. But the greatest of these is love.

NT–6 Ephesians 5:2a, 25–32

This is a great mystery, but I speak in reference to Christ and the Church.

Brothers and sisters:
Live in love, as Christ loved us
and handed himself over for us.
Husbands, love your wives,
even as Christ loved the Church
and handed himself over for her to sanctify her,
cleansing her by the bath of water with the word
that he might present to himself the Church
in splendour,
without spot or wrinkle or any such thing,
that she might be holy and without blemish.
So also husbands should love their wives
as their own bodies.
He who loves his wife loves himself.
For no one hates his own flesh
but rather nourishes and cherishes it,
even as Christ does the Church,

because we are members of his Body.
For this reason a man shall leave his father and his mother
and be joined to his wife,
and the two shall become one flesh.
This is a great mystery,
but I speak in reference to Christ and the Church.

NT–8 Colossians 3:12–17

And over all these put on love, that is, the bond of perfection.

Brothers and sisters:
Put on, as God's chosen ones, holy and beloved,
heartfelt compassion, kindness, humility,
gentleness, and patience,
bearing with one another and forgiving one another,
if one has a grievance against another;
as the Lord has forgiven you, so must you also do.
And over all these put on love,
that is, the bond of perfection.
And let the peace of Christ control your hearts,
the peace into which you were also called in one Body.
And be thankful.
Let the word of Christ dwell in you richly,
as in all the wisdom you teach and admonish one another,
singing psalms, hymns, and spiritual songs
with gratitude in your hearts to God.
And whatever you do, in word or in deed,
do everything in the name of the Lord Jesus,
giving thanks to God the Father through him.

As well as these Bible readings, your minister may be happy to include a suitable non-religious reading and choices have been as diverse as passages from *Winnie the Pooh* and *Captain Corelli's Mandolin*!

Alternative Bible readings

God creates women and men to look after the earth (Genesis, Chapter 1, verses 26–28)

A love poem between two lovers (Song of Solomon, Chapter 2, verses 10–13; Chapter 8, verses 6 and 7)

Jesus teaches how to live life that brings true happiness (Matthew, Chapter 5, verses 1–10)

Jesus teaches about marriage, and welcomes children (Mark, Chapter 10, verses 6–9 and 13–16)

What happens when Jesus attends a wedding reception? (John, Chapter 2, verses 1–11)

Love, actually! (1 Corinthians, Chapter 13)

Committing to each other (Ephesians, Chapter 5, verses 21–33)

Seeing the good side (Philippians, Chapter 4, verses 4–9)

Getting the perfect relationship (Colossians, Chapter 3, verses 12–17)

Being a good lover! (1 John, Chapter 4, verses 7–12)

Grace

If you decide to invite your parish priest to the reception – which is often the case with couples who attend marriage preparation courses and where a strong bond has been created – you may wish to ask him to say Grace before dining.

Here are some samples of Grace that may be said by the priest, or alternatively by a guest, if the priest is not attending the wedding.

Father we thank Thee for this food,
for health and strength and all things good.
May others all these blessings share,
and hearts be grateful everywhere.

(Traditional, circa 1800s)

Some hae meat and canna eat,
And some wad eat that want it;
But we hae meat and we can eat,
And sae the Lord be thanit.

(Robert Burns)

Our Father in Heaven,
We give thanks for the pleasure of gathering together for this occasion.
We give thanks for this food prepared by loving hands.
We give thanks for life, the freedom to enjoy it all.
And all other blessings. As we partake of this food,
We pray for health and strength to carry on
and try to live as you would have us.
This we ask in the name of Christ Our Heavenly Father.

(Harry Jewell, mid-1900s)

For what we are about to receive
may the Lord make us truly thankful
for Jesus Christ sake. Amen

We thank you, Lord, for happy hearts,
for rain and sunny weather;
we thank you for the food we eat,
and that we are together. Amen

Thank you God for blue skies over me,
Green grass under me,
Good friends beside me.
Thank you God for good food in front of me
And peace all over the world. Amen
Thank you for the world so sweet,
Thank you for the food we eat,
Thank you for the birds that sing,
Thank you, God, for everything!

Civil ceremonies

In 1994 the Marriage Act changed civil marriages thus enabling them to take place on premises approved for the purpose by local authorities. Marriage could then be solemnized in registration districts in which neither party resides. It was no longer necessary to have your wedding at the local register office, which, more often than not was a building of practicality, rather than a romantic setting for a dream wedding! This was an incredibly exciting prospect for couples and venues alike as the flood gates had been opened and hundreds of venues applied for licences enabling them to conduct civil ceremonies on their premises. Stately homes, hotels, museums and so on are all now able to host both the ceremony and the reception, which makes a wedding so much simpler for any couple; if they choose not to have a religious ceremony, their civil marriage can take place at the same location as the reception, eliminating any transport problems and the time involved in travelling from one place to another. A list of the approved venues can be obtained from your local register office, or the General Register Office website (see Taking it further: Useful organizations).

You are required to give Notice of Marriage at your local register office and once given, your notice is displayed at the office for a period of 15 days.

If the notice is given on the 1st December, for example, the marriage can take place from 17th December onwards, with the notice being valid for 12 months.

The minimum legal age for getting married in England and Wales is 16 years, although if one partner is under 18, he/she must have a written letter of consent from a parent or legal guardian.

Top tip

When you first approach your local registrar to check availability, it is wise to provisionally book him/her for your chosen dates until you are able to confirm with both the venue and the registrar. This avoids disappointment, especially if your wedding is to take place during the most popular summer season.

The format for a civil ceremony

Once you have decided to opt for a civil ceremony, you have a wealth of choices before you, with regard to the arrangement of the service. The registrar will have been booked to perform the legalities, but the rest is entirely up to you, to discuss freely with your chosen venue.

Readings for a civil ceremony

Unlike a religious church ceremony, civil ceremonies are not permitted to contain any material which relates to a particular faith. Therefore, when choosing your readings you may opt for a more personal approach by writing your own 'vows', which you can recite to each other, either by memory or by reading them on the day. There are some wonderful excerpts from plays, books and pieces of poetry that you may use to enhance the romance of the ceremony.

Top tip

Your chosen readings should be shown to your registrar before the ceremony just to ensure that they are of suitable material; you do not want any problems on the day, with refusals or problems that may cause unnecessary upset.

Blessing For A Marriage

May your marriage bring you all the exquisite excitements a marriage should bring, and may life grant you also patience, tolerance, and understanding.

May you always need one another – not so much to fill your emptiness as to help you to know your fullness. A mountain needs a valley to be complete; the valley does not make the mountain less, but more; and the valley is more a valley because it has a mountain towering over it. So let it be with you and you.

May you need one another, but not out of weakness.
May you want one another, but not out of lack.
May you entice one another, but not compel one another.
May you embrace one another, but not out encircle one another.
May you succeed in all important ways with one another, and not fail in the little graces.
May you look for things to praise, often say, 'I love you!' and take no notice of small faults.

If you have quarrels that push you apart, may both of you hope to have good sense enough to take the first step back.

May you enter into the mystery which is the awareness of one another's presence – no more physical than spiritual, warm and near when you are side by side, and warm and near when you are in separate rooms or even distant cities.
May you have happiness, and may you find it making one another happy.
May you have love, and may you find it loving one another!

(James Dillet Freeman)

Apache blessing

Now you will feel no rain, for each of you will be the shelter for each other.

Now you will feel no cold, for each of you will be the warmth for the other.

Now you are two persons, but there is only one life before.

Go now to your dwelling place to enter into the days of your life together.

And may your days be good and long upon the earth.

Treat yourselves and each other with respect, and remind yourselves often of what brought you together.

Give the highest priority to the tenderness, gentleness and kindness that your connection deserves.

When frustration, difficulty and fear assail your relationship – as they threaten all relationships at one time or another – remember to focus on what is right between you, not only the part which seems wrong.

In this way, you can ride out the storms when clouds hide the face of the sun in your lives – remembering that even if you lose sight of it for a moment, the sun is still there.

And if each of you takes responsibility for the quality of your life together, it will be marked by abundance and delight.

Loving Somewhere

Somewhere between friends
came conversations touching
new ways of seeing each other

Somewhere beyond admiration
eyes met and looks lingered
And the moment shimmered with magic;

Somewhere between laughing and liking
barriers fell away and two souls met
revealing secrets and dreams

Somewhere beneath
the sharing and the smiles
the warmth and the words
there emerged love.

(Source unknown)

The Art of a Good Marriage

The little things are the big things.
It is never being too old to hold hands.
It is remembering to say 'I love you' at least once a day.
It is never going to sleep angry.

It is never taking the other for granted;
the courtship should not end with the honeymoon,
it should continue through all the years.

It is having a mutual sense of values and common objectives.
It is standing together facing the world.
It is forming a circle of love that gathers in the whole family.

It is doing things for each other, not in the attitude of duty or
sacrifice, but in the spirit of joy.

It is speaking words of appreciation and demonstrating
gratitude in thoughtful ways.
It is not expecting the husband to wear a halo or the wife to
have wings of an angel.
It is not looking for perfection in each other.
It is cultivating flexibility, patience, understanding and a sense
of humour.

It is having the capacity to forgive and forget.
It is giving each other an atmosphere in which each can grow.
It is finding room for the things of the spirit.
It is a common search for the good and the beautiful.

It is establishing a relationship in which the independence is
equal, dependence is mutual and the obligation is reciprocal.
It is not only marrying the right partner,
it is being the right partner.

(Wilfred Arlan Peterson)

A Reading on Marriage

When you find someone you can love and who can love you, then love one another. And, as you love one another, remember this: Make your love a joyous, freedom-loving adventure. Let your love be a moving sea between the shores of your souls. Sing, dance, and be joyous together, and yet, let each of you have moments alone. Let there be spaces in your togetherness so that the winds of the heavens dance between you.

Remember, the strings of the lute are together, yet alone as they quiver with the same music. As the pillars of the temple stand apart, they serve a common goal. Fill each other's cup, and yet, allow each to drink at their own choosing. Give one another of your bread, while allowing each to season it to their own taste.

Give your hearts to each other, while providing space for each other's heart to be free, for there is much in life to be loved. Let your lover's heart be free to answer the call of life.

Stand together, yet not too near each other, for in the garden of life, the oak tree and the cypress each have air to breathe and a little earth to call their own, where the sun can reach down and touch them bringing forth the hidden beauty that lies within each one. Yes, be together, and be yourself. Be free, and always be together.

(from The Prophet *by Kahlil Gibran)*

Commissioning a poem

Poets are in demand for today's weddings as couples want to personalize the vows used at civil ceremonies; they would prefer to use words that mean something special to them, rather than churn out well known readings that have been read time and time again. The poet will ask for as much information from the couple as possible, so that he/she is able to tailor the prose to their individual clients. Perhaps a poem could be commissioned to send out as a thank you to guests for attending the wedding and printed on scrolls, or placed into mini frames as a unique keepsake.

Poetry companies will write original 100 per cent bespoke poetry to captivate and show your heartfelt sentiments through prose. Whether a sprinkling of humorous anecdotes, an overriding message of love or a trip down memory lane, poets are able to produce a personalized poem to cherish and give as the gift of a lifetime. The Poetry Studio suggest that 'a beautiful rhyming prose could be created to give as a thank you gift to parents, a retrospective look at the wedding day for yourselves, after the event, or even printed and sent out to guests as a keepsake'. The poetry can be presented in a variety of ways, such as framed with a montage of your photographs, or uniquely displayed on a canvas print, with a selection of your chosen wedding prints arranged as a montage under the poem to create a stylish piece of contemporary artwork, tailored and colour-matched to complement the interior of your home.

Civil partnerships

On 5th December 2005, The Civil Partnership Act 2004 was passed, which allowed same-sex couples to register as civil partners of each other from the 21st December 2005. This was a major step forward for gay couples and the journey began to gain equal legal rights as opposite sex couples. A civil partnership is a completely new legal relationship, exclusively for same-sex couples, distinct from marriage. The Government has sought to give civil partners equality of treatment with spouses, as far as is possible, in the rights and responsibilities that flow from forming a civil partnership.

What are these new rights?

Partners can: access joint treatment for income-related benefits; joint state pension benefits; they have the ability to gain parental responsibility for each other's children; they are recognized for immigration purposes and are exempt from testifying against each other in court. In addition, should one partner die the other will have the right to register their death and claim a survivor pension. They are eligible for bereavement benefits and compensation for fatal accidents or criminal injuries. Surviving partners are recognized under inheritance and intestacy rules and will have tenancy succession rights.

Civil partners are able to accrue survivor pensions in public service schemes and contracted-out pension schemes from 1988.

Civil partners will have the same rights as heterosexual couples and will be treated in the same way as spouses for tax purposes. These changes will be dealt with in the first available Finance Bill.

There are a small number of differences between civil partnership and marriage. For example, a civil partnership is formed when the second civil partner signs the relevant document, and a civil marriage is formed when the couple exchange spoken words. Opposite-sex couples can opt for a religious or civil marriage ceremony as they choose, whereas formation of a civil partnership will be an exclusively civil procedure.

Gino and Mike Meriano, Directors of Pink Weddings were the first gay couple to marry in Brighton, England, at Brighton Register Office on the 21st December 2005 at 8a.m. They were asked if they would like to accept this honour as they have been campaigners for many years, working with councils to try and help the community and the only gay social enterprise to be praised in Parliament for their work towards same-sex couples' rights. Their website (www.pinkweddings.eu007) supplies a wealth of information from lists of suitable venues, including National Trust properties in England and Scotland, top ten hot spots and overseas weddings. Although gay couples are not able to have a legal civil partnership ceremony in many European countries, it is still possible to have a legal ceremony here in the UK and then have your celebratory event in the form of a Blessing Commitment Ceremony in a romantic setting abroad. Gino suggests venues such as: 'Fabulous baroque-style venues in Venice, medieval castles in Tuscany, overlooking Lake Geneva in Switzerland and chic Prague, all of which have their own dedicated local representatives, with good sound knowledge of the area, who can advise and arrange your perfect day.'

On 20th July 2005 the Canadian government introduced legislation to allow the marriage of same-sex couples. Gino says: 'We are now able to organize legal ceremonies in this stunning country, as this law also applies to tourists travelling from abroad. Marriage licences are obtained through any municipal office in Ontario, signed by both parties and once the relevant paperwork has been submitted, the process is relatively simple and the licence remains valid for up to three months. A wedding can then take place in a number of venues, with a popular location being the Rocky Mountains where you can be married outside by a tranquil frozen lake, a waterfall, or even be transported by helicopter to the top of a remote mountain top to exchange your vows.'

Term 'marriage' in civil partnerships

At the time of publication it is not yet possible to use the term 'marriage' when it relates to a same-sex couple as the law states that: 'A marriage is a union between a man and a woman' and therefore gay weddings are termed Civil Partnerships.

Registering the partnership

A couple is required to give notice before registering the partnership in England and Wales, either in a register office or in an approved premise.

This notice for each person states the following:

- name and surname
- date of birth
- condition (marital or civil partnership status)
- occupation
- nationality
- place of formation.

The notice is displayed for a period of 15 days, after which the civil partnership can be registered. The notice is valid for 12 months. The minimum legal age for registering is 16, but individuals under the age of 18 must have written consent from a parent or legal guardian.

Humanist blessing

The first Humanist wedding ceremony was performed on 18th June 2005 and has been recognized as legal in Scotland since 1st June 2005. However, these blessings, as they are often referred to, are still not recognized in England and Wales and therefore couples who do not reside in Scotland would usually choose to employ the services of a Humanist Celebrant to add an additional, more personal dimension to the official marriage. These blessings are also popular to celebrate other life-cycle ceremonies, such as baby naming and memorials.

Humanist vows

The Humanist blessing would be designed and tailored to the individual's personal wishes, in conjunction with the Society of Humanists (www.humanism.org.uk) or the Scottish Humanist Society (www.humanism-scotland.org.uk). One of the main advantages would to be able to write your own special vows, such as this example:

I (name) promise you, (name)
that I will be your (wife/husband) from this day forward,
to be faithful and honest in every way,
to honour the faith and trust you place in me,
to love and respect you in your successes and in your failures,
to make you laugh and to be there when you cry,
to care for you in sickness and in health,
to softly kiss you when you are hurting,
and to be your companion and your friend,
on this journey that we make together.

Second marriages

It is a sad but true fact that one in three marriages end in divorce. However, it is encouraging to learn that nearly half of all wedding ceremonies performed involve individuals on their second marriage. This must mean that as a whole, divorcees want to try marriage again and will marry their second partner in a bid for happiness. One explanation as to why we have such high divorce rates is that as a modern society we have greater values for marriage than in the past, and expect more from a relationship; when it fails we want to move onto new and happier partnerships.

Of course, divorce is not the only reason to enter into a second marriage. Widows and widowers will often want to remarry in order to find a companion with whom to share their life.

The second marriage is usually performed as a civil ceremony, held in an approved premise, with the emphasis generally on a less formal affair. Often the couple's children take the part of a bridesmaid/pageboy, or ring bearer and the bride often chooses not to wear the full bridal gown; instead she may opt for an outfit which she could wear again, such as an evening gown of soft feminine design, or perhaps a suit.

It is possible to remarry in church, however it is at the discretion of the minister and each individual case is considered on its own merit; couples should approach their local church/minister for advice.

Marrying abroad

There are many tour operators specializing in weddings abroad who will deal with all the relevant paperwork on your behalf. Exotic, far-flung destinations have become increasingly popular with couples who want to combine the luxury of a tropical island wedding with a perfect honeymoon paradise to enjoy after the formalities.

The professionals will be able to deal with any queries and will have local representatives in the country of your choice who are able to liaise between the venue and yourselves for all the arrangements and services, such as organizing the wedding cake, transport, flowers, reception and accommodation.

Tour operators

Some of the most popular destinations for weddings abroad are Mauritius, St Lucia, USA, Barbados, Antigua, Jamaica, Sri Lanka, South Africa and Thailand.

Top tip

The local knowledge of the representative at the hotel/venue abroad is invaluable and is key in the smooth running of the event. Having said that, the majority of these establishments – although very experienced – are nevertheless extremely busy with back-to-back weddings in the peak season and it can sometimes seem that there is a lack of individuality in the services offered to a couple. Therefore, should you require anything out of the ordinary, it would be advisable to leave sufficient time to allow the rep to source your request.

- If you have chosen to take just a small gathering of close family and friends abroad, other friends and family members left behind often feel excluded from the proceedings and so you may decide to try to arrange a second celebration on your return.
- Marriages in foreign countries are recognized in the UK if they do not contravene the laws of eligibility in the UK. If there is any doubt about the legal standing of a marriage advice should be sought from the Home Office before any travel arrangements are made.
- It is also advisable to consult a doctor at least three months before leaving to find out which vaccinations and other medical precautions, such as malaria tablets, are necessary.

Most tour operators will request photocopies of the legal documents required to forward to your destination, and the originals should be taken with you on your journey.

Legal requirements

Ensure that you have discussed every detail with your tour operator. If necessary, check with the Embassy or Consulate to double-check the legal requirements; for example, there may be a required minimum period of stay in the country before the ceremony and documents may be required such as birth certificates, passports and evidence of single status (divorce documents, or a death certificate of former spouse for people entering second marriages). There is also usually a minimum residency requirement. In the USA, some states require a blood test before a wedding can take place, and in Bali couples have to belong to one of the five religions that are recognized by the government.

A wedding in Antigua

This is an example of the legal requirements for a wedding in Antigua:

- original birth certificates
- valid ten-year passports
- full names, addresses, occupations and religions of the bride and groom
- full names of both sets of parents (if not on birth certificates)
- if single – affidavit obtained in Antigua from authorized solicitor declaring single status
- if divorced – decree absolute with court stamp
- if widowed – death certificate of former spouse and previous marriage certificate
- if name has been changed by deed poll – legal proof stamped and signed by a solicitor. This also applies if a married woman has reverted back to her maiden name
- if adopted – the adoption certificate
- if aged under 18 years – parental consent in the form of statutory declaration stamped and signed by a solicitor
- minimum residency before wedding – three working days.

Combining a wedding abroad with a church blessing

Some couples choose to have the legal ceremony abroad with close friends and family and when they return, organize a church blessing followed by a party for all those who could not attend the wedding abroad.

Marrying a foreign national

If one of you is a national of a country outside Canada, Australia, New Zealand, South Africa, the EU or USA, the church has a responsibility to conduct marriages that will be recognized in the country from which the couple originate. It is therefore advisable to consult the relevant Embassy and obtain a letter to state that your marriage will be recognised and if marrying in a church, it should be by Common Licence, rather than Banns.

Asian weddings

Anita Patel, Director of Tania-Tapel, runs an Asian Wedding Planning business and says that the Asian wedding market can be significantly more complex and expensive than its Western counterparts. At an average cost of £25,000, the increase is largely due to the vast number of guests invited and the subsequent catering and venue costs. She says: 'To have an organized approach from the beginning will bring you no end of dividends. There are some key decisions that need making and being decisive will certainly help, although with Asian weddings the input of so many people means you need to be prepared to listen. Once you make a decision try to stick with it because, ultimately, too many changes will lose you credibility, not just with your family but with suppliers too.' One of the main differences between a traditional British wedding and an Asian celebration is the involvement of the extended family in the preparations. Usually in a Western marriage, it is the bride and groom who will make the majority of the decisions. An Asian wedding typically involves additional input from both sides of the family, plus siblings, uncles, aunts and grandparents in some cases. The Asian wedding market is growing all the time, reportedly worth £300 million a year and as the culture dictates the importance of marriage it is therefore a natural progression. Indian weddings continue to be large affairs with many hundreds of guests, although Anita says: 'Indian weddings traditionally used to have up to 2000 guests and be completely chaotic, without any structure or order and with all the problems arising from catering for such huge numbers and lack of management in both the preparation stages and on the day. Thankfully, modern Asian couples realize that it is necessary to plan ahead and employ professionals to co-ordinate the proceedings and today the average number of guests is more likely to be 200–400, which is certainly more manageable.' Some Asian couples are scaling back the large numbers to a greater degree, opting instead for a more intimate event of a higher quality, rather than diluting the event to accommodate family and friends who perhaps are not particularly close.

The customs and traditions of the Indian culture are still practised at weddings within the UK, with several celebratory gatherings prior to the wedding day, including the engagement and Henna parties (when the women get together and their hands and feet are decorated with Henna products in traditional bridal designs). The day itself is centred around the ceremony and the importance of the food served afterwards. The formalities differ from religion to religion. For example, the Muslim groom is sat in one room with the offer of the hand in marriage and the acceptance of the bride done in another room. Once legally married they will usually make a grand entrance together, perhaps led by a Dhol player (drummer) and sit on a throne in front of their guests to enjoy the reception and take blessings from guests. Most British venues are not equipped to serve the specialized cuisine required for an Indian event and therefore outside caterers will be employed by the family to provide the four starters, six main courses and two to three desserts that make up the wedding breakfast. This lasts an incredible four to six hours.

The wedding cake is traditionally sponge, which is a firm favourite, with eggless vegetarian sponges also on offer nowadays to cater for the Hindu marketplace.

Each religion has dietary traditions that are adhered to during the main meal in the day. For example, a Hindu Gujarati wedding will have no meat or alcohol served at lunch; however, for the evening reception many modern Asian Hindu Gujarati couples relax the rules somewhat to include meat options and a bar will serve alcohol to those who enjoy a tipple! Dancing is very popular and will last for many hours, with entertainment provided by Baja bands, jazz musicians playing Bollywood music, classical sitar, tabla performers and DJs. Finally at the end of the evening, the Doli (or leaving ceremony) takes place. This significant part of the day symbolizes the bride leaving her maternal home and joining her husband's new household. This is generally a very emotional time, with friends and family bidding their farewells as the couple go off to enjoy an evening of playing games at the husband's family home – a gesture of welcoming their new bride; uniting both families is paramount at any Indian wedding.

Top tip

Tania-Tapel suggests: 'Sit down with both families from the beginning to ensure you get a feel for what everyone wants – including finalizing numbers – or you may find that you waste a lot of time planning something that just may not be what is acceptable. Save time and effort by listening, compromising and coming to a common conclusion ... this is a union of two families and not just two people.'

In this chapter you will learn:

- **which venue to choose and why**
- **what questions to ask when booking a venue**
- **suggestions for venue ideas**
- **sources of venue information**
- **about marquees**
- **about wedding venues abroad.**

A crucial decision

Choosing the venue for your wedding reception is the most important and often most difficult decision in the planning of your wedding, as it will dictate the style and format for the whole day. Many factors will determine the location; for example, if the church is in an area where there is little choice of suitable venues, you may have to travel some distance to find your ideal place. Transport arrangements will then have to be taken into consideration and possibly overnight accommodation for guests. If you are having a civil ceremony you may then choose to book a venue for both the marriage and the reception.

The local register office in the area where the church or civil ceremony is taking place will have a list of venues that are available for wedding receptions, so this is a good place to start your search.

There are approximately 20,000 venues for hire in the UK, some of which are located in incredibly exciting settings. These range from the most magnificent manor nestled in the midst of the British countryside, to the intimate surroundings of a private city bijoux hotel, offering luxurious accommodation and dining in style.

There are pros and cons to all venues and it is very rare that you would be able to find the absolute perfect combination so you may have to compromise. Therefore, when making appointments for a viewing, it is crucial to ensure that you have covered all aspects of their services and you have asked the relevant questions for your particular requirements.

Questions to ask the management at the venue

- How many can they accommodate for a civil ceremony?
- How many can be seated for a wedding breakfast?
- Is dancing permitted and if so, are there any restrictions on the type of music allowed? (For example, the venue may be in a residential area and have an outside terrace where only certain types of music may be played, such as harpists, classical trios/quartets, but not amplified music.)
- Are you able to have access to the venue/room the day before or earlier in the day as you may need time to decorate?

- Until what time can alcohol be served? Some venues have their licence until midnight, but if the venue has residents, it is usually later; however, it is possible to apply for an extension to the licence.
- Can you have naked flames in the venue? Some English Heritage and National Trust properties do not allow candles due to the fire risk and damage to paintings and so on.
- What time do you need to vacate the premises?
- Do you have exclusive use of the venue or will there be more than one event (wedding) held on the same day? Unfortunately there are some venues who allow more than one wedding to take place on the same day, and it has been known for two brides to meet each other in the bathroom, or for guests to wander into the wrong room and start mingling with complete strangers! Obviously this is not ideal for anyone, especially for the couple as they want to feel that it is their special day instead of being part of a conveyor belt system. If you have exclusive use, the charges are usually higher, but they will include any accommodation available and therefore you may be able to spread the costs between your bridal party and any guests who need to stay overnight.
- Does the venue require you to book all the rooms whether you need them or not?
- What are the room layouts? Will there be sufficient space for dancing to begin straight after the meal, or will guests have to move to another room while the dance floor is laid? If so, is there a suitable space for guests to congregate?
- Will there be staff continuity? Often the turnover of staff in the catering trade is quite frequent and the discussions you may have held with one Banqueting Manager in September may not be adhered to by a new manager in the following summer. Therefore it is imperative that you keep copies of all discussions and agreements between yourselves and the management so that you are able to ensure that any requests are duly noted and confirmed in writing.
- If the ceremony is not taking place at the venue, you need to carefully consider the length of time it will take to get to the venue from the church and if it is any longer than half an hour, you should arrange transport for guests (perhaps with drinks on board) so that they arrive refreshed and relaxed.
- If the venue has an outdoor area (for example, a terrace or lawn where you intend to serve a drinks reception), discuss your options with the management, as you will need a contingency plan should the weather be inclement.

- What are the Terms and Conditions of the venue? For example, if you confirm numbers one week before and they decrease on the day, will you be liable to pay for the original estimate?
- If you book accommodation at the venue, will the bridal party and family be upgraded? Are there any perks for the bride and groom (complimentary bridal suite, champagne, chocolates)?
- Are there any preferential rates for a midweek event? Often hotels catering for the corporate client will need the business at the weekend and will offer more favourable rates than leisure hotels that will have clients booked over the weekend and do not therefore need an event to fill their rooms.

City weddings

Cities such as London offer a huge variety of venues, from elegant addresses with stunning banqueting suites and attentive staff to cater to your every whim, to modern hotels with smart, funky decor and contemporary lighting for a more relaxed, informal celebration.

If outdoor space is important, there are a limited number of venues with courtyards, gardens and terraces that you will be able to utilize for a drinks reception, many with beautiful views over the parks and gardens of the city.

The time of year that the wedding will take place will direct you to the best possible options to make the most of the facilities. For example, a stylish hotel with a wonderful crescent-shaped room with floor to ceiling windows, leading out to an Italian garden terrace overlooking Knightsbridge, which guests are able to enjoy, may be perfect during the summer months, whereas a venue with its warm inviting atmosphere, rich oak panelling and log fires is perfect for a winter wedding.

London and other cosmopolitan cities have a plethora of interesting alternative venues in which to hold your celebration, including: museums, galleries, restaurants, riverboats and private town houses.

Styles of city venues

- A luxurious five-star Grade II listed building in the heart of London, built in the grandeur of the Victorian era. It offers elegant, spacious surroundings with the spectacular Winter Gardens on the ground floor, an impressive area, with 20-foot palm trees stretching up to the atrium. This would be the perfect venue to celebrate a stylish wedding and with the benefits of city parkland nearby, it is a photographer's dream.

- Hidden in the heart of the city, a conservatory boasts lush tropical foliage, housing finches, quails and exotic fish.
- Get married on board one of the most famous sailing vessels in history. Legal marriage ceremonies are not permitted on moving vessels, however this ship is safely moored and would create a wonderful themed wedding venue for swashbuckling adventurers aboard this breathtaking Tudor galleon!
- A stunning sleek ship would be a wonderful venue for a nautical-themed wedding reception. With the feel of a private yacht: contemporary teak decking, leather and bespoke weave carpets and a striking glass grand staircase in the centre leading to a breathtaking open air teak deck and champagne bar on which guests would be able to enjoy a drinks reception while watching the city pass by!
- Not many people can boast that the Royal Family have been at their wedding, and these are only a few of the rich and famous who could be part of your special day if you choose to hold your reception among the waxworks of a famous museum.
- Many riverside gastro public houses in the city are very popular venues for the more relaxed informal wedding reception. Have fun transporting your guests by boat to the docklands where they will disembark and find themselves entering a piece of history where Lord Nelson entertained Lady Emma Hamilton in the room upstairs and whose name was derived from a cannon fired to celebrate the opening of the West India Docks in 1802.

Theatrical weddings

Two famous London theatres have opened their doors to the wedding market and licensed their premises enabling them to host civil ceremonies. The London Palladium and The Theatre Royal, Drury Lane are now both available for civil marriages and civil partnerships.

Country weddings

The British countryside is a wonderful setting in which to hold a romantic wedding, with its wealth of historic properties offering superb views over magnificent gardens and estates.

If you are fortunate enough to live within reasonable distance of a stunning rural location, and if it is within your budget, you would be well advised to visit the local venues early on in your arrangements, as the most popular days (Saturday and Sunday) in the summer will be booked far in advance – sometimes even years!

Although the image of your guests sipping champagne on the lawn of a majestic castle maybe your idea of heaven, unfortunately the British weather tends to be somewhat unpredictable and therefore there should always be a contingency plan available for inclement weather. More often than not venues will have an alternative area indoors that can be used for the drinks reception should the weather turn unpleasant.

Some venue organizations offer their properties exclusively to wedding clients, which is advantageous as not only do they understand the particular needs of the bridal party, but they will only accept one wedding per day, making your wedding a very special, personal event.

Styles of country venues

- Imagine a Tudor mansion being the exclusive venue for your wedding, complete with lakes, beautiful parkland and a sweeping driveway.
- Castles can offer falconry, archery and exciting outdoor activities to guests staying prior to and after the wedding.
- Historic Grade II listed buildings, Pump Rooms, lighthouses and other similar attractions around the country host wedding ceremonies and receptions for the more adventurous client.
- How about your own personal island, only accessed by boat with picturesque white-washed bridges and waterways offering exclusive use for your own private celebration?
- A converted medieval Norman church lost in the countryside lit only by candles and braziers, with a stone floor strewn with herbs, would fill your hearts with the magic of such a romantic location.

Scottish weddings

Scotland can boast some of the most romantic locations in the UK! The laws for getting married are also more relaxed, as marriage ceremonies are able to take place anywhere, including in the open air, as it is the minister who is authorized to perform the legal requirements and not the venue itself. At least 15 days and up to three months notice must be given at the register office in the district where the wedding is to take place. A venue nestled on a sandy cove, with incredibly beautiful views across the Loch to the peaks of Ben Lomond, is an ideal backdrop for a truly memorable celebration.

Top tip

- To make your wedding day really special, choose a venue that offers exclusive use so you and your guests can really relax and enjoy the day.
- Make sure your venue has plenty of bedrooms for guests wishing to stay overnight. Not only is this convenient for guests at the end of the evening but you can then meet up for breakfast the next morning and talk about the day.
- Ask your wedding venue if they have anywhere for the bride and bridesmaids to stay the night before the wedding. This way, you can arrive the evening before and relax and pamper yourselves ready for the next day.

(For addresses and contact details see the 'Taking it further' section at the back of this book.)

Sources of information for venues

The internet

The days of having to call individual venues, requesting brochures and visiting each and every one before you made a decision has changed dramatically with the introduction of the internet, providing a vast amount of information on sourcing a wedding venue. Prior to even requesting any literature, you are now able to go online, view prospective venues and often have a virtual tour of the rooms and grounds, which will give you a good indication of their suitability. However, photographs and even video footage can be misleading and venues that look incredibly luxurious and spacious can in reality be much smaller and less illustrious than the image portrayed online. Therefore, do not rely solely on this glossy first impression, as nothing will ever replace the importance and value of a personal visit to your short-listed venues, in order to meet management, have a good look round and gauge whether it is right for your particular needs.

Wedding Venues and Services magazine

Together with the bridal magazines, another source of valuable information is *Wedding Venues & Services* magazine published quarterly, which is both inspirational and packed full of helpful ideas and all the latest topical wedding news. It provides its reader with an A–Z of hundreds of wedding venues in the UK, categorized by county, with good quality photographs and useful sample menus. It has other useful details on individual venues nationwide, such as:

- Is it licensed for civil ceremonies?
- What is the price range?
- What is its capacity?
- Does it have outdoor facilities?
- Is there a bridal suite available?
- What parking is available for guests?
- Is a kosher menu offered?
- What type of cuisine is available?
- What accommodation is available for guests?
- How many functions are held at any one time?
- Does the venue have an in-house party planner?
- Are outside caterers permitted?

These are all vital questions that you need answers to and this magazine will save time in your search. It also has regular features on different styles of wedding venues, new approved premises and current trends. With regular features on castle settings, barns, or grand hotels with stunning ballrooms, you are sure to find all the information you need to make an informed choice and find your dream location! It also has a useful website (www.wedding venues.co.uk).

Register office

Register offices will have a list of all licensed venues in your area which can be sent to you or accessed online and they will be able to advise on the style and location of most of them over the phone; many registrars have first-hand knowledge of the majority of their venues, having conducted numerous civil ceremonies in their locality, so it is often a good idea to have a chat with the registrar before setting out.

Marquee weddings

A wedding in a marquee can be a fun, glamorous and exciting experience, however it also has the potential for disappointment as unfortunately there are still companies that continue to trade offering inadequate service and quality. If a company has not been recommended by a valued friend, you would be well advised to visit a few different organizations to ensure that you are fully aware of all the options available to you.

Site visit

When approaching a marquee company for a quotation, it is advisable to arrange a site meeting, at a venue where a marquee has already been erected, ready for a function. This way, you are able to see the quality of the canvas for yourself and witness a completed marquee with all the decorations, lighting and furniture *in situ*.

Once you have found a company who offers the style and quality you are looking for, there are a vast array of choices to make in order to complete the interior. However, before the decoration of the marquee can be decided, the location has to be considered.

Perhaps you plan to erect the marquee in your parents' or a friend's garden, or you may have access to a plot of land adjacent to your property? If this is the case, the marquee supplier will arrange a site visit when he will be able to assess the suitability of the location and advise the necessary requirements. For example, you may need to trim any overhanging foliage or branches from nearby trees, or there may be a need to level the ground, or construct stilts under the marquee to support the flooring.

Venue recommendation

If you choose to have a marquee wedding reception in the grounds of a stately home, or private house, the venue will often provide a list of recommended marquee specialists, as they will have used these companies on a regular basis and will be able to guarantee their professionalism. This will make your job easier, as it will take away the uncertainty of using a new company.

Styles

Marquees are generally of a framed construction with a plain white outer PVC covering and a pleated lining (usually ivory or white) which provides a neutral backdrop for theming the space. You should be offered a choice of colours for the interior lining valances, to match your chosen colour scheme. If it is a summer wedding and the weather is glorious, most marquees have window walls that can be elevated to reveal the surrounding countryside and let in some fresh air. Doors can be Georgian or Gothic, wooden or aluminium and the flooring can be wood or carpeted throughout for a warmer feel. During the winter months the marquees are heated.

Interiors

The furniture and lighting is generally arranged by the marquee company, which is the simpler option, although always ask for a breakdown of costs so that you know how much you are paying for each item, as they vary considerably. For example, chairs come in a huge variety of styles and some are more expensive than others; this also applies to quality of napkins and tableware. The supplier will provide lighting, usually in the form of chandeliers and heating, such as blow heaters, for inclement weather.

Marquee decoration

As with other venues, it is possible to decorate the space in a marquee to your own personal taste and theme. There are extremely competent companies specializing in designing and creating unique and elegant transformations, using stylish linings, decorative overlays and innovative décor to enhance and create impact. With the help of a professional's skill and knowledge, it is possible to completely change a blank canvas into a warm, inviting Moroccan kasbah: brass lamps and lanterns can light tables draped with deep, rich maroon covers; using gold chairs and low seating with exotic scatter cushions and for an earthy atmosphere, filling the air with Moroccan spices, intoxicating your guests with the romance of the desert!

In contrast, you may prefer a clean, simple décor: masses of soft white drapes, painted with beautiful butterflies, hung above tables adorned in cool, crisp white linen; tall glass vases holding a single white hydrangea and an aluminium curved bar serving champagne from frosted crystal.

Alternative marquees

Traditional white canvas marquees, with ruched linings have been popular for many years. However, there has also been an increase in demand for an alternative outdoor construction that is unique and adaptable to a more individual taste. Tent and marquee suppliers have recognized this need and new innovative companies are able to supply a comprehensive collection of beautiful tents, marquees and crafted structures. MD Charles Preston of LPM Bohemia says: 'A 'yurt' is often used as an alternative structure for weddings. This uniquely beautiful onion-domed pavilion is made from a range of oiled hard woods, is fully waterproof and is an elegant blend of global architecture and cultures and is versatile enough to accommodate between 100 and 500 people dining. On a balmy summer's evening, the walls can be opened and the centre cap removed to allow the warm breezes to flow through. Mini versions of these yurts are available to be used as additional accommodation for your guests! Why not party the night away in a themed pavilion, lined with Persian rugs, sumptuous Arabian lounge seating, and exotic cushions, transporting your guests back 2000 years to the days of the Arabian Nights and then retire to your own personal luxurious pavilion alongside other guests in the open air and enjoy the pleasures of a bohemian tent at night.' Other suggestions could include a more rustic vibe, reminiscent of village fetes and cream teas, using a hard-wearing vintage tent, faded by 60 years of British sun. Or perhaps recreate period scenes from yesteryear, a M*A*S*H-style field hospital tent.

The weather

The weather plays a huge part in the degree of success of an event, but unfortunately, it is the one factor that no one can control – even a Wedding Planner! However, there are ways of being prepared for the best or the worst of weather by consulting websites that provide accurate information about likely temperatures and chances of rain weeks in advance (www.wiseweather.co.uk). You will then be able to prepare for any rainy weather by providing umbrellas for the bridal party and guests if there is to be a considerable distance between buildings, or by constructing a suitable covered walkway. The caterers will need to ensure that they have adequate heating provisions during a cold spell, or air conditioning for example, if it is to be a scorcher!

Wedding venues abroad

Weddings in far-flung destinations evoke images of romantic evenings with close friends and family witnessing your vows being exchanged as the sun sets on a secluded tropical beach, or of you being serenaded by a steel band as the palm trees sway in time with Caribbean music as you toast each other's health with champagne under the stars! These are the images we have been used to, but today the idea of marrying abroad has taken on new dimensions with Europe being a very popular destination. Italy and Spain are proving particular favourites, as they involve a relatively simple legal process, compared to other European destinations – such as France – which have a much more complicated system.

Here are a few suggestions for some romantic destinations. See bridal magazines for topical ideas and features on many other fabulous places.

Italian weddings

There are a few dedicated wedding specialists organizing marriages abroad and these companies offer bespoke services tailored to your individual requirements. Italy offers rich cultural locations, beautiful lake and mountain views. Rosa Spatola, Director of 'Weddings in Italy', advises that there are no residency requirements for Italy, but clients should try to arrive in the country a few days before the ceremony in order to confirm last-minute arrangements. In certain areas of Italy, it is also possible to have a civil ceremony in the open air, even in the cobbled courtyard of a fifteenth-century villa.'

Cortona

Cortona houses a thirteenth-century town hall, complete with exquisite frescoes in the city's main square and has an ancient and medieval feel. Another is the Villa San Crispolto, an impressive chapel that also boasts old-world frescoes for your Protestant wedding in Italy.

Ballegio and Sorrento

Ballegio and Sorrento are frequently visited by couples wanting to get married in the south, as is Sicily, with its stunning beaches and aqua waters. The number of British couples deciding to marry in Italy has increased over the past five years, with some companies organizing over 500 weddings a year! One of the reasons why Italy is often chosen above other European locations is the cost, as it is incredible value for money, considering the average cost of a wedding in the UK!

Rome

A wedding in Rome would encompass a city of exquisite architecture, history and the some of the most romantic photo opportunities in the world! Just imagine how you would feel posing in front of such renowned wonders as the Trevi Fountain, the Colosseum, St Peter's Basilica and the Sistine Chapel – they would certainly fill your album with a wonderful collection of photographs. As Rome is the city of St Valentine, the patron saint of lovers, it has countless Catholic churches and basilicas, some dating back to the Byzantine period. It is the only city with three civil town halls, one which would encircle your guests by the Roman Forum and the masterpiece of the Piazza del Campidoglio square, designed by Michaelangelo.

Italian lakes

If a city wedding does not appeal, why not choose an idyllic location on one of Italy's superb lakes, such as Lago Maggiore. Here you will find the most perfect hotels and restaurants perched on the banks of a stunning lake, with reflections of the mountains in its glass surface – the most wonderful setting for a marriage, perhaps with a champagne reception on the lawn at the edge of the lake, and only the passing swans to ripple the waters.

French weddings

Frank Damgaard, Director of Monte-Carlo Weddings advises that: 'There are strict guidelines to residency laws for couples wanting to tie the knot in France prior to the marriage, and the couple have to live in the area for 40 days before an application can be made to the local Town Hall (Marie) for a licence. However, if you or your family have any property in France, this rule may be relaxed somewhat, so it is very important to contact the Mayor of the town where you plan to have the ceremony and ask his/her advice on your own particular circumstances.' Only civil ceremonies in France are legally binding and therefore if you would like to have a religious ceremony, you must have a civil ceremony first. Ceremonies can take place in a number of incredible venues in the principality of Monaco and the French Riviera. Some venues include: a medieval castle, with stoned walls and set in beautiful gardens or a luxurious villa with vistas over the Riviera. Imagine white-washed gazebos erected around a stunning swimming pool, lit with floating candles and fresh flowers. For the legalities of marrying in France contact:

General Consulat in London
21 Cromwell Road
LONDON SW7 2EN
Tel : (44) 207 073 1200
Fax : (44) 207 073 1201
www.consulfrance-londres.org

Caribbean weddings

Couples have been marrying in tropical destinations and combining their weddings with a romantic honeymoon in far-flung resorts for many years. Caribbean islands have always been very popular, some of the most fashionable being Antigua, Jamaica, St Lucia and The Bahamas. Each island has its own documentation and residency requirements and a specialist travel operator will be able to explain these in detail.

Regulations of marrying in Jamaica

- Residency requirement – 48 hours
- Documents required – state-issued birth certificate
- All pages of all court-certified final divorce decrees if a second marriage
- State-issued death certificates with related marriage certificates for those remarrying after the death of a former spouse

- Legal name change or legal adoption documents if applicable
- All legally translated documents must also be notarized
- A notarized sworn affidavit referring to documents specifically should also be provided to accompany photocopies of documents
- Original/certified documents are also accepted, however, documents will not be returned
- Notarized photocopies (with the notary's original INK signature and stamp) of the required documents for both the bride and groom must be sent via courier at least 60 days prior to the arrival date.

Residency requirements for other Caribbean islands

- St Lucia – 3 full business days
- Bahamas – 48 hours
- Jamaica – 48 hours
- Antigua – 48 hours

Resort weddings

Specialist travel operators are continually updating their packages to cater for the more discerning couples and have extended their services to include luxury themed weddings, where you are able to choose from a collection of unique designer items to personalize your day. Celebrity designers have joined forces with Wedding Planners and tour operators to offer a selection of upgrades for flowers, tableware and decoration in the various packages. They promote themselves as ensuring that each wedding is tailored to the individual's needs and although they perform innumerable wedding ceremonies in the same resort per day, they assure us that couples will not feel that they are part of a wedding machine; they take care to make each wedding very special, by scheduling timings very carefully and by using a number of locations around the resort to hold the ceremonies. However, it is important to discuss these issues with your operator and make sure that you are fully aware of the nature of weddings in resorts and the potential for privacy and the intimacy of the occasion to be compromised by the sheer volume of the ceremonies taking place on any one day!

New York weddings

More couples are choosing 'The city that never sleeps' as the venue for their wedding than ever before! There is a wide and varied selection of ceremony and reception venues to choose from, including quirky gallery spaces in Chelsea and hip lofts in Soho, not to mention the tallest and most famous Fifth Avenue landmark building, the Empire State Building with its 55th floor wedding suite which attracts many British couples! Following the ceremony, arrangements can be made to take a World Yacht Dinner Cruise, a helicopter ride, a horse and carriage ride through Central Park or even arrange a personal message flashing in neon lights above Times Square.

However, at the time of publication New York has not yet legalised civil partnerships, so same-sex couples are not able to have their partnership sealed in the city.

Why choose New York?

Gemma, a British bride who recently married in New York, dreamed of a wedding with panache and style. As her husband-to-be, photographer Scott, was familiar with the city, they decided to employ the services of an American Wedding Planner – with offices in the Empire State Building – recommended by their travel operator. Just three days after they arrived with their close family and friends, they were officially allowed to marry, and a ceremony was organized in a private area of Central Park, known as the Conservatory Garden. The rich autumn colours of the park's foliage and the crisp blue skies, were perfect for the outdoor ceremony performed by a local reverend at the edge of a water fountain. Following the ceremony, they were whisked off in a New York cab to the ferry port where a private motor launch was waiting to take them to a restaurant on the water's edge, overlooking the magnificent New York City skyline. Gemma sourced this venue on the internet and made all the reservations direct with the restaurant, which has a dedicated wedding team to deal with enquiries.

Top tip

If you are doing your own research into wedding venues abroad, it would be advisable to choose well-established and experienced establishments, who are able to show a record of their quality and culinary achievements and who are recognized in the industry. If at all possible, make time to visit the venue when arriving in the country to finalize details and reassure yourselves that it is suitable for your requirements.

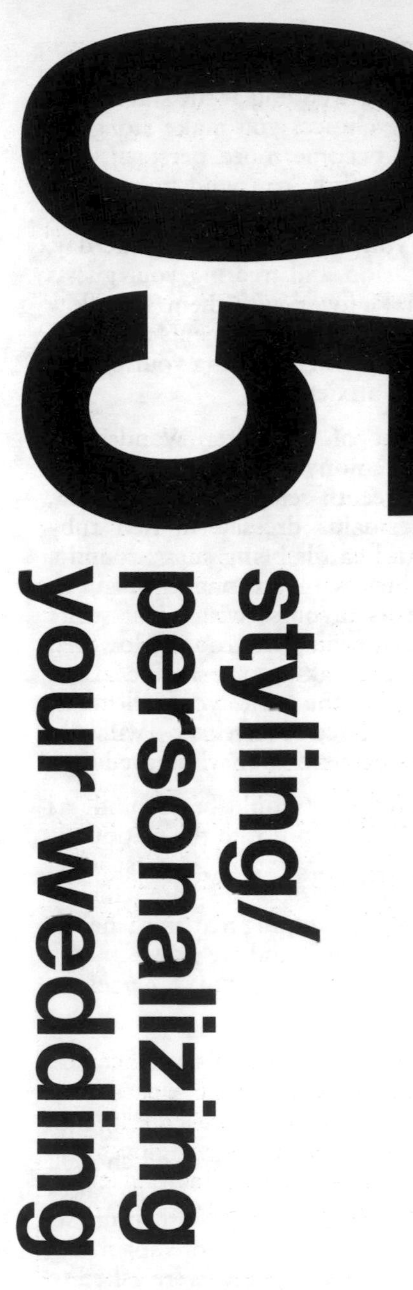

In this chapter you will learn:

- how to decide on your theme
- suggestions for themes/styles
- the pros and cons of DIY planning versus a professional organizer
- lighting advice
- venue decoration
- place setting ideas.

Choosing your theme

Deciding on a theme or style for your wedding at the start of the arrangements will help to ease the choices you make along the way. Increasingly weddings have become more personal, and couples are able to let their imaginations run wild, to create a completely individual event. By giving just a little extra thought to every detail of the wedding, you will be enriching the day, making it a uniquely special occasion and treating your guests to some wonderful memories to take away with them. Do allow yourself sufficient time to source the various elements to ensure that you have the optimum degree of fun designing your perfect day, without any undue stress and anxiety!

Perhaps you have always dreamt of a Winter Wonderland wedding, with a charming ceremony taking place on a December evening, in a quaint fifteenth-century village church, full of flickering candles, bridesmaids dressed in rich ruby velvet, with fur-trimmed muffs and carols being sung around a roaring log fire. Christmas baubles with the names of guests etched in glitter could be given as favours, with silver white sprigs of birch, lit by fairy lights adorning the room. However, if you are struggling with a concept, making one small decision – for example, choosing the colour of your flowers, bridesmaids' dress fabric, or even a piece of jewellery – will help to inspire a wealth of ideas to co-ordinate your whole wedding.

If you choose to theme your wedding, it could be as subtle as incorporating your favourite butterfly motif into the stationery, wedding cake and tablecloths, or as extravagant as persuading all your guests to dress as Bond characters, as they are whisked off to the reception in flash sports cars, sipping martinis (shaken not stirred!) while you and your new husband are flown in by a hair-raising helicopter stunt! Here are some popular themes, as food for thought!

Beach heaven

This is an amusing choice if you are having a summer wedding in the garden. A couple who met on a surfing weekend chose a beach theme; they created a sandcastle of fairy cakes individually decorated with shells and pebbles, gave their guests miniature buckets filled with fresh fish and chips for supper and served ice cream in cornets for desert. The guests were asked to join in the spirit and dress in appropriate attire, with the women in sun dresses and the men in Bermuda shorts! Dancing took place on the 'beach' terrace lit by bamboo torches, and revellers boogied to tunes by the Beach Boys all night.

Romantic fairytale

A bride's fantasy of recreating the Cinderella story saw her dressed in a replica ball gown, complete with diamanté tiara and drop-pearl earrings, riding off in a glass coach with white horses – with her 'Prince Charming' in doublet and hose – to a fairytale reception at a picturesque castle, nestled in the heart of a wooded glen. A feast was laid on for the gathering, and the proceedings culminated in a spectacular midnight display of fireworks.

King Arthur's Camelot

You could start by designing the invitations in the style of a scroll, written in calligraphy, sealed with wax and tied with a velvet ribbon. Guests could be asked to dress in medieval costume, or for those not as comfortable wearing the whole regalia, perhaps suggest that tones of gold, royal blue and purple should be worn. The top table could resemble King Arthur's round table, draped in black and silver linen, with the best man and ushers as Knights of the Realm and the bride and groom drinking from pewter goblets! The venue, if not already of the period, could be themed with tapestries hung from the walls (patterned rugs, or patterned fabric to cut costs), candles burning on heavy iron candelabra, and suits of armour as props around the room.

New Orleans jazz and casino

Hiring a Mississippi Paddle Steamer to transport your guests along the Thames after the ceremony would instantly create an atmosphere of being back in the nineteenth century in the Deep South, with entertainment by a New Orleans jazz band, and guests enjoying the novelty of a strolling magician to baffle and amuse them. Guests could mingle before dinner on the upper deck, followed by dancing, and enjoy hours of fun gambling at the American Roulette and Blackjack tables, served by costumed croupiers.

Reality check!

Needless to say, the majority of weddings tend to be less theatrical affairs, and although it is wonderful to have a tantalizing imagination and a clear vision of how you would like the most important day of your lives to be, do not forget that somehow your dream has to be turned into a reality. It may be possible to achieve your expectations, budget and time permitting; however, you may have to compromise, due to factors beyond your control – such as venue regulations and restrictions, or weather conditions – so be prepared to be flexible and open to alternative solutions to prevent any disappointment. Having said that, a wedding is a wonderful opportunity for you to have a great deal of fun and really enjoy incorporating some of the more quirky elements of your personalities, be it hobbies, aspirations or passions.

Proficient professionals or determined DIY?

Professional theming

If you have a set theme and are fortunate enough to have access to a substantial budget, you may want to employ a professional company to style and decorate your venue. Perhaps you have imagined hosting your wedding reception in the depths of the English countryside, but complicated travel arrangements or other issues may restrict your choice. Therefore why not recreate the grandeur of a stately home, with its glorious gardens, fountains and sculptures, in the heart of the city! A central gazebo, embellished with trailing ivy and fairy lights, furnished with elegant garden chairs and sumptuous cushions, could be the centrepiece of the reception, with guests being entertained by a classical string quartet softly playing in harmony with the rhythmic sound of the Italian fountains. Transforming a blank canvas into your dream setting is the forte of a number of event companies, with the assistance of props, backdrops, lighting, staging and – above all – manpower.

Managing Director of Juno Productions, Emma Bewick works with both technical crews and wedding planners and says: 'Concept and design is the easy part, the tricky part is ensuring that everyone involved is happy: from the most important people being the couple, and of course their immediate family, right through to the wedding co-ordinators, the venue management and the production team. Often, the bride and groom will choose everything that contributes to their wedding, such as the menu, the table plans and the type of flowers they desire, but a production team are there to put things in the right positions, continuing a fluid theme and adding unique and eye-pleasing effects.'

It is possible to decorate the venue without the help of a professional. However, bear in mind that these companies have the innovation, flair and vision required for the task and although you may have unbounded enthusiasm, it is always an extremely time-consuming and labour intensive exercise and careful thought should be taken before you commit yourselves. It would not be recommended unless you have some willing friends or family who could spare the time and energy the day before the event to carry out the makeover and it would be advisable to ensure that these willing volunteers were not playing any major roles at the wedding!

Pros and cons of DIY versus professional

- Using a professional will provide the ideas and manpower necessary to create a complicated theme.
- A professional will add an additional cost to your budget and will need to be considered carefully if you are to employ a production company.
- Doing it yourself will save costs and given the ideas, time and manpower, it is possible to achieve a good result.
- Always allow plenty of time in your schedule for theming, as it will always take longer than you had anticipated.

Illuminating your day

Church and reception lighting

The lighting at both the church and reception is crucial and will often make or break an event. It is very important and must be conducive to the atmosphere of the wedding, in order to achieve the ultimate ambience throughout the day. Dull, badly-lit churches will leave the congregation uninspired; fill the shelves and altar with masses of tall ivory candles, flickering softly and their mood will lift with the rousing hymns.

Outdoor lighting

For a winter wedding, why not place bamboo torches along the path outside the church so that guests are led away by a dramatic aisle of flames? Tiny fairy lights fed through an ornate display of gorgeous blooms around the arch of a doorway, would be a spectacular entrance to a romantic ceremony.

A torch could be lit either side of the main entrance to greet your guests at the reception; how about intertwining lights in the bracken and hedges of a stately home, to gently light the terrace as dusk arrives, or suspend lanterns with scented tea lights from trees and shrubs to fill the atmosphere with aromatic fragrances?

Table lighting

Lighting each table individually in the room with a pin spot will add drama and emphasize the centrepieces, although these can be expensive to hire in if the venue does not have this facility.

To complete the look, the walls of the room could also be lit, by swathing them with muslin and lighting the cloth from behind. Bands and discotheques will sometimes supply their own starlight cloths as a stylish back drop; however, these can be hired if they do not have their own.

Candles

Warning: never leave candles unsupervised when children are around.

Candles placed in floral arrangements on the tables, standing alone or within tea light holders, will enhance any venue, or use floating candles in a glass bowl to illuminate and introduce a beautiful glow.

Top tip

Try to purchase the best-quality candles as possible; the cheaper options will burn quicker and will have to be regularly replaced or the wax will melt into the petals!

Lighting on a budget

Fairy lights are one of the most effective, yet inexpensive methods of lighting on the market. Go for dramatic impact by lighting tree trunks and branches with hundreds of sparkling white lights to delight your guests later in the evening (ensure you have purchased outdoor lighting and that the transformers are placed indoors). Create a fairytale canopy on the ceiling by linking strands of lights to a central point in the room – for example, a chandelier – and then bring them back out to the walls, in a web-like fashion, transforming a bland room into a palace fit for a royal ball!

Tables tops and co-ordinating chairs

Tables

Once you have chosen your venue, there are many ways to personalize the space, one of the most effective being to dress the tables. Your guests will be spending a large proportion of the day sitting down during the meal and will be perusing their surroundings while chatting to fellow diners. Therefore if the tables are fun and interesting, reflecting the theme, they will not only be a great source of pleasure to look at, but will become a talking point with your family and friends, and all your hard work will be appreciated and savoured by each and every one of them.

Chairs

Chairs also play an important role in the overall look of the room, especially if you choose to have a sit-down meal, when there will be a greater number used. If the venue has their own chairs which do not suit your scheme, why not hire your own for a relatively low cost, with co-ordinating seat pads, or consider opting for chair covers to match your colour palette (a somewhat more expensive choice)? An alternative option would be to drape organza or tulle around the existing chairs, tied with a bow, a sprig of ivy or sweet scented lavender for a stylish finish. This will consolidate the theme and add interest to the room.

You may be restricted by the constraints of the existing colours of the walls, carpets and soft furnishings of the room, but do not let this hurdle prevent you from achieving the ambience of the day.

Top tip

If the venue has an unsightly and brash colour carpet, cover it by sprinkling fabric rose petals all over, cleverly disguising an unwanted pattern and shade, with the least amount of expense and effort – just make sure you are not the one sweeping them up at the end of the day!

Dressing your tables

Tablecloths and napkins are available to hire in a vast array of colours and fabrics to complement your design. Crisp white damask linen cloths provide a neutral backdrop for your floral arrangement; apple green table runners, with gingham napkins arranged on pale lemon cloths will lend themselves to a spring theme; pretty pinks, lilacs and baby blues will evoke images of a warm summer evening spent mingling with guests, sipping glasses of chilled champagne.

Top tip

If the venue or your budget restrict you to plain cloths, drape some sheer fabric such as organza (or a less expensive substitute such as voile) over them and scatter fresh rose petals on or underneath, for a touch of romance. Fabric can be purchased at most department stores and haberdashers. Table confetti in all shapes and sizes is available to liven up your tables; you can even print your own image onto heart shapes – there are a huge variety of designs to amuse your guests!

Chic crockery and gorgeous glassware

Specialist crockery and glassware can be hired to adorn the tables, although there will be an additional hire charge if you choose not to use the caterer's own equipment. Stylish black oriental chinaware and chopsticks, would be wonderful if you were serving sushi. Pretty floral, or polka dot crockery and fluted cake plates stacked high with iced fairy cakes, would be ideal for a sophisticated Afternoon Tea reception, while simple, pure white tableware and cut glass is perfect for a classic, polished style.

Top tip

Bridal magazines are a wonderful source of ideas and suggestions for table decorations and regularly print beautiful glossy photographs of inspirational room settings, with seasonal colour schemes.

Perfect place settings

Once your seating plan has been finalized, for a formal sit-down meal, there are an abundance of methods to ensure your guests know where they are to be seated. Of course, tables could be numbered, which is a rather traditional way. Alternatively:

- You could opt for a more modern trend and design each table sign to tie in with your theme. For example, the signs could be cut in the shape of Greek islands for a couple spending their honeymoon cruising around the Mediterranean.
- Use titles of poetry books (with excerpts printed on the back) for the romantics who met in a library.
- Incorporate the names of your favourite songs, printed on oversized bass clefs!

The seating plan

The seating plan is often designed to suit the style of the wedding, by decorating it with flowers and foliage to blend in with the decor, or stunning shells for a beach look and draping the easel/stand with sheer fabric, or strands of ivy. There are innovative suppliers who will even design the plan on clear perspex, giving the illusion of your guests' names engraved on a piece of glass – a real showstopper!

Unique place cards

The printing of the place cards and seating plan may be done by a professional stationery company. However, there are countless fabulous, original ways of indicating a seating arrangement to charm and thrill your guests.

Everyone loves chocolate, so treat your guests' senses by ordering name place holders in solid chocolate etched with your names in soft red hearts or a design of your choice to co-ordinate. How delicious to indulge in eating your place setting after the meal! These can also be used as favours and are available in original, stylish and unique designs, each one handmade using the finest Belgian chocolate.

One of the simplest and least expensive techniques is to slip a handwritten card into a linen napkin wrapped with a sprig of ivy. This is extremely effective and although quite time-consuming, gives a very stylish and classic look.

Top tip

If you are gathering the ivy from your garden yourself, make sure you wash it carefully and leave to dry before you tie it on the napkin; otherwise it will leave a dirty mark on the linen.

Confetti

Today there is an incredible range of petal confetti to purchase over the internet or from specialized shops. Hand-picked roses, bougainvillea, peonies and even orchid blossoms, dried naturally to keep them looking fresh and vibrant, are available in many colours for scattering everywhere. Tables benefit from a sprinkling of these fragrant petals and more couples are choosing to supply their guests with cones constructed from handmade paper, filled with real petal confetti, to be thrown at the church. They are the preferred alternative to rice and standard paper confetti which have traditionally been used, and as they are completely biodegradable, the church ministry is usually happy to accommodate this option in their churchyards. However, I would recommend that you double-check before distributing them to your guests, so as not to cause offence if there is an objection.

Other companies offer fabric petals with the opportunity of having your names printed on them and bridesmaids often enjoy being given a pretty basket full of them to scatter in front of the bride's path as she walks down the aisle; but once again, check with your clergy for his permission.

A fun suggestion for the young at heart is to blow bubbles at the couple's exit from church, or at the end of the ceremony. A full range of bottles (personalized if required) are sold through various outlets and are generally non-staining – a very important safeguard should any bubbles settle on the bride's dress!

Favours

A centuries-old custom of giving your guests a small gift to take home began in Europe, with the French *bonbonniere* (favours), and the Italian version of confetti, a keepsake usually comprising of five sugared almonds wrapped in circlets of tulle, symbolising fertility, happiness, wealth, health and longevity. The Italians create elaborate bouquets from clusters of sugared almonds made into the shape of petals and give decorative silver ornaments to all their guests. The cluster of five sugared almonds used to be very popular with UK weddings in the 1990s, but have been replaced with more innovative, fun and personal gifts. It has even become fashionable to give your guests a lottery ticket each – with the proviso that any jackpots must be shared of course!

Funky favours

Some of the following suggestions can double-up as a place setting, by attaching a name tag tied with a piece of co-ordinating ribbon or raffia.

Photo mugs	printed with a love poem, funny quote or a line from your wedding vows
Chocolate bars	personalized and labelled – can be used as place setting
Cookies	sealed in cellophane bags and tied with pretty ribbon; baked in the shape of the wedding theme: cakes/hearts/flowers/top hat etc.
Jars of honey	printed with labels: 'Meant to Bee!', 'Love is Buzzing!', 'Sweeter than Honey!'

Words of wisdom

Honey was a symbol of fertility, love and beauty in early Greece.

In Greek mythology, Cupid was said to have dipped his arrows in honey to fill the lover's heart with sweetness – what a perfect sentiment!

Miniature photo frames	use these to send to guests as a 'Save the Day' reminder, or as place settings, with their names in the frame
Sachets of hot chocolate	for the chocoholic, personalized with sayings such as 'Blended with Love', 'A Perfect Mix'
Jars of chutney/hot sauce	personalized labels with the bride and groom's name and date of the wedding
Chopsticks	engraved with the wedding date
Miniature galvanized pails	in pastel shades; these can be filled with sweets, cherries, or sand for a beach theme, or sachets of seeds for a country wedding.

Words of wisdom

Seeds are given to symbolize the beginning of something wonderful – perfect for a spring wedding. They emphasize the thought that as flowers need nutrients to grow healthily, so a marriage needs nurturing to be strong.

Favours on a budget

Of course it is not necessary to give your guests anything at all to take home; however, a small thank you for sharing your special day is always appreciated. To cut costs, why not bake some small fairy cakes and ice them with the name of your guest, presented in a cellophane bag and tied with a pretty ribbon, which will double as a place card and delicious gift in one.

Try to buy favour items wholesale; the closer you get to the manufacturer, the cheaper the overall price. If possible buy off season, as the professionals do, so if you are having a winter wedding, be organized and look around in the spring or summer – you could save pounds.

Top tip

Whatever gift you decide to buy, assemble or embellish, enlist the help of friends and family as part of the enjoyment of personalizing your special day, particularly if you have a large number of guests. Remember that everything always takes longer than you would imagine, even with a few extra hands, so allow sufficient time.

Balloon decoration

Balloons can quickly transform a simple hall into a fun, colourful and impressive venue. Large spaces can easily be filled with helium balloons strategically placed in gathered arrangements, or perhaps opt for a dramatic spiral arch display at the entrance for guests to walk through! It is possible to buy the balloons yourself and inflate them using a hired gas cylinder, and although time-consuming, if you do have sufficient time in your schedule, you will be able to decorate the venue with simple arrangements at a relatively low cost, with the supplies being provided by local specialist outlets. For those weddings where the budget is greater, specialist decorating companies are able to take the workload off your shoulders by producing a whole range of theming options. Your designs can be as ambitious as your imagination allows, with elaborate displays and arrangements including heart sculptures, freestanding arrangements and even balloon pyrotechnics! Imagine the drama and impact you would create on the dance floor by having a giant balloon suspended above, filled with 100 small balloons, which exploded just as you both were taking the floor for your first dance, showering you with fluttering confetti.

Top tip

Andrew Yeates, of the Balloon and Kite Company says: 'By choosing only two colours, you will achieve a much subtler look to complement your scheme, although if you are going for a psychedelic 1970s hippie theme, multicoloured balloons would be perfect.' He also advises not to inflate the balloons until the day of the event, as helium filled latex balloons only last one day, and unless you use the foil balloons you will find them deflated by the time the wedding day arrives.

Happy snaps

An amusing trend is to leave single-use cameras on the tables for your guests to take impromptu snaps of each other while dining. Some of the funniest, most candid shots of your album could include those taken by friends and family during the festivities, capturing moments you might otherwise have missed. Just remember to allocate an usher or bridesmaid to collect the cameras at the end of the day and keep them safe, or have them developed so they are ready on your return from honeymoon.

Impressive ice

Ice sculptures add impact and excitement to a room and although they tend to be a relatively costly item, due to the techniques and labour involved, they will guarantee the wow factor at your reception. Sculptures may be designed to your individual brief, as was a recreation of the Eiffel Tower for the bride whose groom proposed to her at the very top of the real thing on Valentine's Day, or the three-tier wedding cake made of ice, cascading with fresh strawberries. The standard designs, such as interlocking hearts, and swans are also very popular. However, if your budget does not stretch to such an extravagant addition, perhaps you could still introduce a smaller design into your scheme, such as an ice punch bowl, which would keep your drinks perfectly chilled, or impress at the buffet table by serving a scrumptious fresh fruit salad from a flower-lined dish carved from solid ice.

Enchanting entrance

Today's couple literally do have the world at their feet! A personalized aisle runner to gild the approach to your wedding ceremony is one of a plethora of services on offer nowadays to the discerning duo. If this rather decadent addition to the day is of interest, suppliers are able to provide standard designs in complementary colours and patterns, as well as bespoke monogrammed creations. It is also a popular choice to scatter the aisle with paper, silk or fresh rose petals. The approach to the ceremony of a July wedding would be wonderfully enhanced as the scent of fresh lavender trodden underfoot permeated the air and treated your guests to the heady aroma of summer.

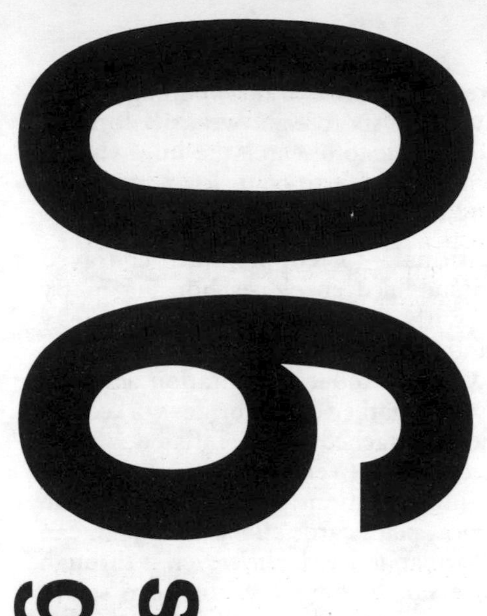

stationery and gift lists

In this chapter you will learn:

- **styles and format of invitations**
- **types of wedding stationery**
- **about stationery on a budget**
- **about traditional gift lists**
- **about alternative and charity gift lists.**

The invitations

The first clue a guest is given of the style of the wedding arrives when they receive their invitation six to eight weeks before the event! It is worth taking some time to research the huge variety of styles available now, which are able to co-ordinate with any colour scheme or theme and will suit any budget.

Styles range from traditional, to copperplate engraved invitations, to gorgeous tissue-lined envelopes housing pretty floral designs and tied with organza ribbon, to wacky caricatures of the bride and groom emblazoned on the front cover in full technicolour! Or how about an invitation designed in the style of a train ticket (the father of the bride worked for British Rail), with a balloon attached to be inflated on the arrival of each guest to decorate the venue. The save the date cards, day invitations, evening invitations, reply and thank you cards, menus, order of service, place cards and seating plan can all be printed in the same format and style; however, if through budget or taste you choose not to have the complete set of matching stationery, you can still co-ordinate all the vital items of information (for example, order of service and seating plan) and perhaps tailor them in your own individual style.

Choosing a company that crafts contemporary acrylic perspex to produce invitations engraved onto clear shapes would be both fun and stylish. Menus for the tables, order of service sheets for the ceremony, napkin rings, name boxes to be used as place cards engraved with the couple's name and wedding date (which would be perfect to double up as keepsakes or favours for guests to take away with them) are all part of the extensive range available. The clear perspex used in conjunction with timeless cream or white flowers and green foliage would produce a stunning design for your reception. For a totally bespoke design, it is even possible to engrave the text of your invitation onto squares of soft leather which roll up into scrolls, for a unique, stylish introduction to a special wedding day to come.

Save the date cards

It has been popular in the US – and is increasingly so in the UK today – to have 'Save the date' cards printed and sent out at the time of the engagement announcement, so that friends and family whose diaries are often booked up many months in advance, are able to make sure that they are free for your wedding. Although an added cost, it makes great sense to ask your guests to keep the day free until you are able to decide on your design and send out the actual wedding invitations.

What to include on the invitation

Once the guest list has been compiled, calculate how many invitations you will need, and always order a few extra of both the invitations and envelopes to allow for mistakes. Most stationery companies will provide sample wording and will send a proof for your approval in plenty of time to make any necessary alterations.

The invitations should include as much information as possible, so that the guest is left in no doubt whatsoever as to what the day holds, with particular importance to the exact location of the church/ceremony and venue, so they are directed with ease. Include:

- dress code – if any
- clear, concise directions
- a map where applicable
- an enclosure to let you know of any special dietary requirements
- printed acceptance card (so that all your guests need do is send it straight back)
- details on local accommodation (a list of local bed and breakfast hotels would be useful)
- parking facilities at the venue.

Civil partnership invitations

Many single-sex couples are keen to purchase specialist stationery designed specifically for celebrating their union in a civil partnership ceremony. There are a number of designers with invitations and other stationery in their collection who meet these needs and whose cards are innovative and fun. For example, a design constructed from handmade paper with two basques, or two dress shirts and bow ties, with the words, 'Ceremony' and 'Commitment'. New companies are entering the market all the time, so check online for details of their stock (see Taking it further).

Evening invitations

These may be sent to guests who are not attending the ceremony but are invited to an evening celebration.

Reply cards

Reply cards are printed with your name and address, so that they can be sent straight back and therefore avoiding any delay in compiling the confirmed guest list.

Thank you cards

These can be of the same design as your theme and sent out as soon as gifts arrive.

Order of Service

An Order of Service sheet or booklet is very useful for your guests to be able to follow the running order of the ceremony. The readings and hymns should be confirmed with your clergy before printing and generally one sheet per couple would be sufficient, with a few extra sheets for the minister/organist/choir.

Order of the Day

An Order of the Day booklet, sheet or card is an additional item to have printed if you would like your guests to take away a memento of the day's events and therefore one per couple with extras for single guests should be allowed.

Place cards

These can be printed or handwritten with the guests' names in a traditional manner, or they may form part of your table design and theme. There are a huge variety of place card holders to choose from, including mini wedding cakes, presents, bride and grooms and hearts, which would make an attractive addition to the table. The cards can be cut in shapes, such as butterflies to blend in with a theme, or tied with ribbons and attached to glasses, napkins or favours.

Menus

You may choose to have menus printed and left on the tables. However, this is an additional option and not always necessary.

Seating plan

Table/seating plans are essential for guiding guests to their tables. They may be as simple or elaborate as you require, with designs on offer to co-ordinate with the theme, in original, novel styles. You may choose to have the plan framed after the wedding and keep it as a memento of the day to remind you of everyone who attended. Check with the venue whether they would print the seating plan, therefore saving costs.

Guest books

Guest books are fun to leave on an appropriate table where guests can make comments, usually humorous, about your wedding day! A suggestion to complement the guest book is to set up a tripod and camera in a quiet area of the venue, where guests can have their photographs taken, and then these can be put into the book alongside their comments to create a fantastic reminder of a very special day.

Stationery on a budget

There are many ways to reduce the cost of printing stationery, which if done through professional companies can be a very expensive aspect of the wedding; by allowing enough time – and with a little creativity – your stationery can be a stylish and very personal. Why not buy some handmade paper, which is available in a variety of textures, including embossed with rose petals, leaves and decorative thread running through it in a spectrum of colours? Print the details of the invitation onto a co-ordinating card in the colour of your theme and mount onto the paper, which can be torn rather than cut, to give a ragged, natural look to a stylish, yet very inexpensive piece of artwork! The same process can be applied to the menus, Order of Service sheets and place cards.

Sample invitation:

KATE AND SIMON

REQUEST THE PLEASURE OF YOUR COMPANY

TO JOIN THEM IN CELEBRATING THEIR MARRIAGE

AT ST LUKE'S CHURCH, CHELSEA, LONDON SW3

AT 2.00PM

AND AFTERWARDS AT

THE DORCHESTER, PARK LANE, LONDON

R.S.V.P.

6 CHEAM COTTAGES

SUTTON, SURREY SM2 4XZ

Gift lists

Friends and family will naturally want to give you a present to mark the occasion and show their appreciation for inviting them to share your special day. Couples used to have to notify guests of their requests discreetly via family members; often this resulted in duplicate gifts or perhaps guests choosing gifts that may have been unsuitable, or simply not at all the couple's taste. This is obviously unfortunate for both parties: firstly for the guest because they have spent money on something that is unfortunately inappropriate and secondly for the couple as they have received an item that they really do not particularly like or need, which would be a great shame. To rectify this, nowadays, the majority of couples choose to enlist the help of a professional gift list company which has many advantages:

- a huge range of gifts available for all budgets
- no duplication
- gifts are delivered – simpler for the guest and bride and groom
- free service for both parties
- couple able to keep track of gifts purchased and send thank-you notes
- generally guarantees are provided for the gifts.

Most large department stores have a wedding gift list service and also operate an online service, for ease of ordering from home. It is also advisable not to restrict yourselves to just one store for your list, but to choose items from several different stores offering a range of practical items as well as the more unique, one-off gifts (see Taking it further).

Charity gift lists

Charity gift lists have become increasingly popular as couples have generally cohabited for a while prior to their marriage and often have already accumulated the majority of their household items and furniture between them over a period of time. Unless you intend moving to a new home which will need furnishing, you may choose to opt out of receiving a wedding gift and nominate a charity instead to receive donations from your guests. This can be done directly through an agency, a gift list company, or cheques can be personally collected by a member of the family through the reply cards and sent to the charity of your choice.

Love, honour and a bray!

World Vision is a charity organization offering an alternative wedding gift service, whereby guests are able to buy gifts on your behalf. These gifts make a huge difference to Third World countries and some of the world's poorest children and their communities, helping them on their journey out of poverty.

Some of the gifts available include: giving a donkey to help families affected by the conflict in Darfur, Western Sudan to rebuild their livelihoods by assisting with household tasks; giving a pig to a family in Zambia to rear and from which they can earn an income, in turn helping to pay for their children's education. You could ask for an 'Emergency cook set' to be sent to a family to prepare their own food and share a meal together during times of crisis such as earthquakes, floods or drought. A window or a door could be bought for a new school being built in Sierra Leone, giving children of all ages access to education after ten years of civil war.

These alternative gift lists could be combined with a more traditional list, so that guests are able to choose whether they would like to donate their financial contribution to charity such as World Vision, or pay for a personal gift for you as a couple.

Alternative gifts

Companies offering 'Experience days' are very popular with guests wanting to give a unique and memorable gift for the couple to enjoy together, and are ideal for those willing to participate in something new. Guests can choose to buy a voucher that entitles the recipients to indulge in an array of new experiences, some perfectly tailored for two people, such as:

- champagne balloon flight and/or anniversary flight
- dinner for two on a Thames cruiser and a ride on the London Eye
- a day out for two driving a Ferrari at a world-renowned race track
- a pampering spa day
- massage workshop for two
- dolphin and whale watching
- a flotation tank for two
- yacht racing for two.

You may prefer to request a contribution towards your honeymoon and therefore you may be given travel vouchers provided by the tour operator.

07 wedding attire

In this chapter you will learn:

- **various options for bridal wear**
- **tips on choosing a dress design**
- **the importance of accessories**
- **how to book a hair and make-up stylist**
- **menswear options.**

Bridal wear

The dress

The dress! The most important choice a bride makes for her wedding day. But which one? What style? Which designer? How much to spend? These are all questions that need to be addressed; however, the most important is how much do you want to spend? Off-the-peg designs can range from a few hundred pounds to a few thousand, however bespoke creations generally start at £3000 and can escalate to anything upwards of £10,000. If you have the funds available to splash out on your dream gown, then who is to say whether you should or shouldn't spend a large sum of money on a dress that you will probably only wear once? A woman's wedding day is one of the most exciting, happiest days of her life and for most brides, what she chooses to wear to celebrate her marriage in front of family and friends – as well as her groom! – is an extremely personal decision. Some will save for many months and spend their hard-earned cash on a one-off designer gown; others will want value for money and opt for a more practical dress (and one perhaps that they can adapt and wear after the wedding). Often there is no option; they simply have to have the best gown they can possibly afford, as they have been dreaming of their wedding day since they were little girls and only the most extravagant creation will do.

The first step is to visit a selection of bridal stores and have fun trying on various styles, colours and fabrics. This will not only be a great day out for you, your mother and girlfriends, but will give you a good indication of what you like and dislike and what may or may not suit you.

Top tip

Do not be put off trying on dresses that you initially think might not be right for you. It is amazing how often gowns look much better on you than on the hanger and vise versa; sometimes the designs and styles you are attracted to immediately do not look as good on you as you might have thought! The one dress that is hanging in the shop that you are not particularly enthusiastic about might very well be your dream dress, or a version thereof, so go on why not try them all!

Hopefully you will receive good, personal and attentive service at the bridal shops you visit. Unfortunately this is not always the case. With the sheer number of women wanting to try on dresses in peak season, it can sometimes become less than glamorous if you are left in a changing room, unable to get yourself out of a huge, frilly, designer meringue of a gown, being left to wriggle and squirm before an assistant comes to your rescue! Not a pleasant experience, but one that occasionally is shared by other brides-to-be in one form or another. Always try to allow plenty of time for your visits, as shops are often very busy and you want to feel well cared for and receive the service you deserve.

A bride told of her experience of booking five very expensive bridesmaids' dresses and her own wedding gown through a well-known reputable company, only to find that once they had received the deposit, their attitude changed and the designers were not as attentive and conscientious as she had hoped. It resulted in all of her bridesmaids' dresses being the wrong size for the varying shapes of the girls, and her own wedding dress – which was presented to her four days before the wedding – was altered contrary to her request, making the dress far too tight. This experience left her feeling angry, frustrated and upset at the prospect of having to wear an uncomfortable gown for the entire length of her wedding day, purely because they had not listened to her instructions and their flippant attitude was very upsetting!

Top tip

Always try to choose a designer and or shop whose service is impeccable and leaves you in no doubt that you will be looked after throughout all your fittings. If not, once you are further down the line with the design, and nearer the date of the wedding, it will be too late to make any changes. Thankfully most bridal wear designers offer a very personal and conscientious service where a bride can look forward to and enjoy all the fittings and fuss made of her at this very special time.

Choosing a design

There are several options available:

- Choose a ready-made design off the peg. These dresses will be available in standard sizes and any alterations (e.g. length of hem or sleeve) will be done by the shop; if not, they should be able to recommend a tailor. This is the least expensive option.
- A dress from a ready-made collection which you may alter to your own specification. For example, if you love the bodice shape but perhaps the skirt of another gown suits you better, you will be able to have the dress made to include the change of design to your own specifications.
- A totally bespoke couture gown is designed specifically for your own requirements. This may be from scratch, meeting the designer initially to discuss the style of gown you had in mind, after which they will make suggestions and sketches to inspire you; this gives the designer an opportunity to understand your likes and dislikes. The process of designing your gown then starts in earnest and generally takes up to six months before the wedding day, during which up to four or five fittings will take place. A toile (a muslin/linen version) will be made of the dress then tweaked and altered according to any thoughts, such as perhaps the neckline is too high, or low, the sleeves need to be tighter, or the bodice a slightly different shape. It is at this stage in the manufacture that the main alterations will be done, before the actual fabric is cut. The cost of couture gowns may start at approximately £3000.

The trend for vintage in the wedding market in recent years continues to spill over into wedding dress designs. Soft feminine Grecian creations in particular are becoming extremely popular. Many brides are now looking for a more comfortable, relaxed wedding gown option, and want to feel feminine without having to dress in a way that may feel over the top and somewhat awkward with the advantage of having a beautiful dress that can easily be worn for many occasions after the wedding.

Accessories

As with all aspects of a wedding, attention to detail is essential and no more so than with the bride's dress and accessories. The finishing touches are vital to complete the look and produce a polished, stylish bride.

Headdresses

An array of headwear is available to the modern bride from fresh floral pieces to funky feathery creations. Choosing accessories to enhance the gown is sometimes difficult as you do not want to overshadow the dress, but at the same time, a few well-chosen pieces will embellish and complete your dream look. Designers are able to create stunning and individual pieces perfectly matched to the style of the bride and her party, simply by working with a sketch of the dress and a sample of the materials. Designer Isabel Kurtenbach says: 'Headdresses complement the gown as do hair pins, tiaras, jewellery and shoes. A wonderful idea to fulfil the 'something blue' tradition is to have a small beaded or crystal flower made to place in your bouquet or hair.' A unique use for tiaras once the wedding is over is to use them as necklaces. Many brides choose not to have certain designs as they feel that they would probably only wear them once and the cost involved may prohibit them from having a piece such as a beautiful tiara. However, Isabel suggests: 'Brides could wear the tiara as a necklace after the wedding, simply by attaching a special chain, and that way, perhaps it could be worn initially on the first wedding anniversary as a romantic gesture and then subsequently at parties, so that it can be appreciated and enjoyed in its own right.'

Such consideration for a client's happiness and satisfaction is paramount in the wedding industry. A bride wants to feel very special in the run up to her big day and as she is investing both her money and time in every single detail of her appearance, she is entitled to a dedicated service, which most dress and accessory designers offer their clients during the months leading up to the wedding. It is always a joy to find suppliers giving good frank advice on whether the style suits their clients, even to the point of turning down a sale if the jewellery or headwear does not look good! Isabel says: 'I can only give my genuine honest opinion and if I really feel that the client would be best with nothing at all, or only one piece instead of the four or five elaborate creations chosen, I will actually refuse to sell them; and they still leave my store, happy, grateful and trusting of my experience.'

Hats

Hats continue to be worn at weddings, although hair accessories, made with beads, crystals or feathers have taken over in popularity in recent years. However, it is traditional for the mother of the bride to look splendid in a co-ordinating hat and if any other guests choose to arrive at the reception in a hat, a way of keeping it pristine, rather than having to put it under a chair, is to display them on a stylish stand, available to hire or made to commission (see Taking it further).

The bride's emergency kit

It is usually the role of the chief bridesmaid to ensure that the bride has everything she may need at the reception, readily at hand. She should arrange to have a little bag of essential items available throughout the day for life's emergencies! These may include make-up, and lipstick in particular – as it will probably be worn off quite quickly during all those romantic photographs taken with your new husband! You may also need to include tissues for during the ceremony, and waterproof mascara.

Hair and make-up

You may have been preparing for this day for a year or more, and deciding which hairstyle and make-up you will have has probably been on your mind nearly as much as what you are going to wear. It is always a wise idea to consider the health of your hair and skin in the run up to the wedding; book a consultation with a hairdresser at least six months before the big day as this allows you time to assess the condition of your hair and if necessary to begin to nourish and prepare it so that it looks its best by the time the date of your wedding arrives. The same applies to your skin; if you try to eat more healthily and drink plenty of water, it will really benefit the tone of your skin, which in turn will produce a fresher, more vibrant complexion, ready for a make-up trial nearer the date.

Booking a stylist

Specialists will be able to pass on a wealth of experience from attending to brides and their families. You will generally first meet your stylist at the 'trial' (see page 99), and have an initial 20 minutes or so consultation to find out everything about the style of the wedding – the flowers, venue, bridesmaids' attire and so on, so that when choosing hairstyles, every aspect is discussed and the perfect look is achieved. If your budget allows, it is a wonderful luxury to employ a hairstylist and make-up artist to come to your house or the venue where you will be getting ready. This decadent indulgence will make a huge difference to the quality and finish of those very important photographs which will be pored over by yourselves – and your friends and family – for many years to come! Like other professionals, good hairdressers and make-up artists get booked up early, so do your research and find someone you can trust and who makes you feel fantastic; then get them to confirm in writing that they will be there on the day. You may choose to use your regular hairdresser to style your hair in their salon on the day; however, bear in mind the possibility of inclement weather conditions and the problem of leaving the salon looking perfect and having to travel back to your house, only to arrive looking windswept and weather-beaten before you have even got dressed! Therefore, to have the convenience of the stylist coming to you and being there for the other members of your party as well, without any hassle, is a great advantage – albeit generally a costlier option.

Booking a trial

In an ideal world, you will have found your team a good few months – possibly even six months – before the date of your wedding, at which time you can discuss the length of your hair and whether you need to try to grow it, or have a particular style cut that will enhance your chosen look. You will then be able to book a trial around a month before the wedding, when it is a great time to take photographs, magazine clippings and ideas you may have for styles and suggestions for your hair. Your hairdresser should then be able to produce several styles at this trial and take photographs for you to peruse and mull over when you go back home, so that you will have time to consider which one suits you and your dress! It is at this trial that you should also try to take along any tiaras, headdresses and veils that you intend to wear, so that he or she is able to give you a full impression of the various possibilities. The stylist may choose to try extensions, hair ornaments or hair pieces, although to change your own style in a very dramatic way is not always wise. It is vital that you are completely comfortable with the way your hair feels and looks; sometimes opting for a totally different 'you' can result in feeling awkward and unsure of yourself – not to mention the reaction of your groom as he sees you for the first time walking down the aisle!

Make-up

Make-up is designed on the same principle as hair and should suit your bone structure and colouring and not leave you looking in the mirror at someone who appears alien to the personality you know so well! However, it is also very important that the make-up is strong enough to highlight your features in the photographs without leaving you looking pale and washed-out. A good make-up artist will be able to judge how much to apply in order to produce a polished, yet natural look, which will enhance your good points and eliminate any problem areas. Sometimes stress and anxiety can cause bad skin reactions and a professional will be able to cover any embarrassing blemishes and hide a multitude of sins!

Top tip

Director of Elle Au Naturel, Antonia advises brides on many aspects of their face and hair. She says: 'Exfoliating is one of the most important beauty treatments to consider. Often brides are stressed and tired when they come for their make-up trial and perhaps their skin is not looking as radiant as they may want. Using a good exfoliator will get rid of all the dead cells and make a huge difference to the lustre of your skin, and therefore the make-up will look so much fresher.' Another really important factor in looking as good as possible are your eyebrows. Antonia says: 'I always insist on my brides having their brows shaped, as it opens their eyes for the photographs and the shadow highlights the brow wonderfully.' As she is a real stickler for timing, Antonia ensures that all her stylists are experts at both hair and make-up, as she feels that this is much more efficient – and there are no issues on the day with one stylist delaying the work of the other.

Make-up lessons

Never book a facial on the day of the wedding or even less than two days before as it will bring out any impurities in the skin and may leave you looking blotchy and red; always book any facial treatments at least a week in advance. Booking a make-up lesson is a great idea for brides getting married abroad who need tips and advice for when they have to apply their own make-up, or for those uncomfortable with having professional make-up applied and would prefer to do their own, with a little assistance beforehand to achieve the best result (see Taking it further).

Menswear

Groom's wear and outfits for the other male members of the party have never been so varied. Gone are the days when only two or three basic designs were available to hire, such as a black pinstripe, grey flannel or a traditional morning suit and top hat. Menswear designers have realized that men today want to look individual and stylish, they prefer to have a wider choice in both hiring and purchasing to complement their bride's attire and are willing to pay more for a quality product.

Groom's wear

With the modern bridegroom becoming more style-conscious, specialist outfitters are providing both suit hire and purchase. Waistcoats are always popular with modern grooms, and pure silk suits in fabulous shades of pale blue, lime green, purple, burgundy, lilac, peach, camel, pink and purple are increasingly the trend, as are the rainbow of pure wool garments in ivory, gold, silver and white.

The styles and ranges available to today's modern groom seem limitless.

Contemporary

Peach or burnt orange pure wool suit with three-quarter length Edward jacket.

Relaxed

For a relaxed, but confident look – rich burgundy silk taffeta.

Silk aspects

A wide palette of shades, with pin-tucks, crushed silks in ivory, white and saffron.

Embroideries

For the special occasion – a silver, silk dupion suit.

Rich velvets

For a rich, vibrant look in soft fine cotton – a deep purple three-quarter length Nehru jacket.

Best man/ushers

The best man and the ushers should wear a suit which co-ordinates well with the groom. However, they will generally choose to be in a less extravagant outfit which blends into the scheme rather than standing out alone.

Father of the bride

The same applies to the father of the bride who should be wearing an outfit which blends well into the colours and fabrics of the groomsmen, with perhaps a matching tie/cravat or waistcoat.

Pageboys

These tend to either be dressed as a 'dinkier' version of the groom, or wearing a completely individual ensemble. With children it is advisable to leave any final fittings to as near the wedding date as possible, as they invariably grow an inch or two; the same applies to footwear.

To buy or to hire?

Bespoke tailoring

There are still bespoke services available from tailors offering individually cut styles to reflect the appreciation of a beautifully-crafted piece of clothing. Discerning groom and groomsmen are able to be visited in your homes or office, by trained measurers, who will help you to choose the cloth and style. Around six weeks later, the suit tailored to your specification will be ready for you to try on, with any alterations having been completed and the finished garment delivered a few days later.

Suit hire

If a bespoke suit is a little over your budget, many department stores situated around the UK provide men's hire services. Their range of suits and accessories are extensive, such as herringbone suits and tailcoats, lounge suits, frockcoats, dinner suits and Scottish kilts. Co-ordinating shirts, such as classic wing collar and dress shirts, are available in adult and children's sizes, with silk ties, cravats, and bow ties completing the look. Waistcoats have always been a stylish way of expressing individuality, and were particularly important at a time when the main part of the suit lacked inspiration. As the choice of designs of waistcoats has increased considerably, they continue to be a mainstay of the groom/groomsmen's outfit and may be bought or hired in a variety of fabrics and shades off the peg. Bespoke, personally commissioned waistcoats are still popular, embroidered with names or designs representing the couple and their personalities. Cufflinks, braces, shoes, a cane, white scarf and gloves, tie pins and even a fob watch are among the finishing touches available.

Asian wear

Britain hosts a huge number of Asian weddings every year and menswear companies have recognized the need for Asian wear to be readily available to clients. Traditional Asian designs include a three-piece full or three-quarter length *sherwani/khuta* outfit with matching pyjama in black, cream or red, with the *khussa* (shoes) and *chuni* (scarves) completing the look.

08 catering

In this chapter you will learn:

- **top tips when meeting the caterer**
- **how to source linen, furniture, glass hire**
- **about sample menus**
- **about wedding packages**
- **tips on drinks at the reception**
- **responsibilities on the day**
- **about the wedding cake and alternatives.**

Meeting the caterer

The catering arrangements are generally dictated by which venue is chosen – for example, if it is a hotel, they will use their own staff for the event. However, if the venue does not have a dedicated catering team on site, it is possible to arrange for your own caterers. Often a venue will have a list of preferred companies that they will recommend to you because they have been used before on a regular basis, have proved to be professional and are familiar with the venue and its facilities. In this case, you should arrange to meet with at least three of the caterers on the list, asking them initially to provide sample menus, so that you can get a feel for the style of cuisine and their costs. Once you have perused the information and had your meeting, you should request a menu tasting, to experience first-hand the quality of both the food and their service.

Top tip

Be cautious of any caterer who is not willing to give a food tasting, as this is a crucial part of the decision process for both parties. It allows time to discuss different dishes and tastes, and provides a perfect opportunity for the caterer to impress with his presentation. You can confirm exactly what you would like before it is put in front of you on the day of the wedding. At this meeting it is vital that all details are covered and that you feel satisfied that all aspects of their service have been clarified.

The modern palate

Long gone are the days when caterers served bland, predictable menus, i.e. melon balls, followed by chicken chasseur, and black forest gateaux for pudding! Catering has advanced dramatically and creative cooking has become what is expected, not the exception! The possibilities are endless: oriental canapés served on dramatic black dishes; sushi bars set up for your guests to try exotic new tastes; mini food is very fashionable, with delicious authentic fish and chips served in newspaper or mini burgers; or break with tradition with afternoon tea served on vintage cake plates.

Special dietary requirements

Your guests' dietary requirements should always be considered. If any special requirements were requested through your replies, hopefully you will be informed of any halal, kosher or particular religious or medical needs that will have to be met. Give the caterer as much notice as possible for these individuals, so that they can arrange a suitable alternative.

Crockery, glassware and cutlery

Ask to see the caterer's range of crockery, glassware and cutlery. Check whether these items are included in the price of the menu, or if they are supplied at an additional cost. If the style is not suitable – perhaps you would like to match a colour scheme or follow a current trend – contact a catering equipment hire company such as Jones who advise that many couples now choose from a range of crockery from classic white, with gold edges, or cream ware to the more unique pewter, oriental dishes or coloured glass plates and coordinating pieces, as they know the significant design difference it can make.' The glassware offered by the caterer is usually of a basic style and this again can be upgraded to a more individual piece, such as a striking blue cobalt water glass, or a Venetian green champagne glass, a martini glass speckled with bubbles or a designer piece by John Rocha or Jasper Conran! Given a limitless budget your tables can look incredibly innovative and spectacular; however, just an extra thought about colours – for example, using an emerald green water glass on the table to accentuate a colour scheme – will add an enhanced dimension to your décor.

Linen

The same applies to the linen being offered by the caterer. There should be a complete breakdown of costs for all the equipment hire and you will be able to calculate and compare the cost of the traditional white linen cloths and napkins against a more interesting fabric or colour, such as a pink and white gingham for a summer wedding, or a striking purple cloth for a medieval winter celebration. Equipment hire companies will also supply linen and furniture for your wedding, and as couples are becoming a lot more adventurous with their choices, it is useful to know that whatever your theme, you will be able to co-ordinate and complete the look successfully by using specialist suppliers.

Top tip

If you choose to change the linen, glassware or crockery provided by the caterer, ensure that if they arrange the new additional items themselves, there is not a significant fee for this service. If so, it is possible to arrange collection and delivery of the new items yourself to save on the budget. However, do bear in mind the time and effort involved, particularly if you do not live near to a supplier's warehouse.

Furniture

Furniture is another consideration, although in most cases the tables themselves are more or less standard and only require a decision on whether to go for round or rectangular. Having round tables for guests instead of the traditional long rectangular styles has become more popular, as it has for the top table as well. This configuration allows guests to socialize more freely and often the bridal party prefer a round table as they feel less on show to the whole room, and people at the ends do not feel on their own! The style of chairs is very important as well (see also Chapter 05 'Styling/personalizing your wedding'). If your wedding is to have the 'wow' factor, there are more exclusive ranges of tables and chairs available to hire, in clear, black and coloured perspex, funky retro designs, benches, sofas, bar stools and bean bags – the list goes on – which will definitely impress your guests! Some hire companies are able to supply wonderfully stylish furniture; however, they often only deal with the trade, and therefore if you have a Wedding Planner organizing your wedding, he/she will have to approach them for costs and availability on your behalf, or alternatively the management at the venue will be able to arrange the booking.

Menus

Most caterers will supply sample menus to show the style of cuisine in which they specialize and although these are only a sample of the ideas they can suggest, they are still a good starting point, offering packages with three course menus including coffee. However, it has become more usual to design a bespoke menu based both on the couples' and their guests' preferences, tailoring the cuisine to each individual's requirements. Today our tastes have become far more sophisticated and we are more discerning in our expectations. The popularity and growth of the TV celebrity chef and the knowledge they have imparted through the media has made us very much more aware of fresh, quality ingredients and good presentation. It is not sufficient for caterers to offer standard, unimaginative dishes any more; we are demanding value for money and delicious innovative creations!

Staffing

Staffing is an important consideration when discussing your wedding with the caterer, as a friendly attitude and professional manner will make the event far more pleasant than if your guests are served by scowling, miserable waiting staff! Good caterers will discuss their staffing practice with you and perhaps show photographs of past events where you will be able to see their uniform and the standard of their appearance. Costs should also be confirmed, as there may be hidden amounts for additional time should the event run later than scheduled and transport/taxi costs may be incurred.

Responsibilities on the day

If you have employed the services of an outside caterer, they should arrange for a manager to be responsible for the running of the event on the day and he/she should be at every meeting, so that communication is thorough and all the key staff are completely confident of their roles and expectations. The same applies to a hotel booking, when ideally you would be able to liaise with the same person throughout the run up to the wedding. Unfortunately, the catering trade is renowned for a high turnover of staff, and it is not always possible to sustain the continuity, which is why it is very important to have the venue/caterer confirm all decisions in writing so there are no misunderstandings.

Avoid any misunderstanding

By asking for written confirmation of every meeting in the run up to the wedding, you should avoid problems. For example, a couple arranged for gold chairs to be available for their wedding breakfast, only to be told by a different member of the venue staff two days before the wedding that they only had red chairs and if they wanted the gold, there would be an additional charge! On another occasion punch bowls had been promised and the couple were telephoned to say that the venue did not have any; again there would be an extra cost if they were required. Unfortunately, if requests are not confirmed in black and white well in advance, these alarming and unnecessary last minute problems can cause undue stress and anxiety.

Organic excellence

The demand for organic food has doubled in the last six years and this is reflected in the choices made for catering for weddings. If you want to be assured of purely organic produce being used for the menu at your wedding, choose a company which is accredited by the Soil Association and able to offer purely organic menus if requested. They should insist on using only the finest ingredients and will often suggest several styles of cuisine to choose from, for example: modern British, European, Moroccan, and French Vietnamese flavours. Matthew Turnbull of Urban Caprice advises: 'Clients should try to have an idea of their budget and the numbers they will be inviting as this enables caterers to respond with creative menus that fit their needs and pockets. Trends are constantly changing in catering, and as couples are becoming more adventurous in many other aspects of the wedding, the food and its presentation are one of the main ways of creating and implementing a strong concept.' If the budget is limited, Matthew suggests that you should be open to ideas on how the day will run and perhaps the traditional timing of a wedding (drinks at 4–5p.m., wedding breakfast at 5–7p.m., dancing at 7–11p.m.) should be reconsidered in favour of a shorter event, with more impact, for example an Afternoon Tea with a menu such as:

Dainty Sandwiches

Duck's egg mayonnaise with land cress
Creamed Yarmouth Bloaters with horseradish butter
Hot-smoked herring paste with a peppery butter
Ridge cucumbers with cream cheese
Wiltshire ham and tarragon mustard

Biscuits and Scones

Piles of Devonshire scones
Ginger parkin
Lavender shortbread
Yorkshire teacake
Milk biscuits
Lemon posit and raspberries served in a tea cup with a silver teaspoon

Jams, Jellies and Creams

Strawberry jam, clotted cream, Pimm's jelly with mint and strawberries and fresh lemon curd will also be served

To quench one's thirst

Lashings of homemade lemonade and fruit infusions

Advantages of a corporate hotel

Local business hotels offering facilities for weddings are a good example of establishments realizing their potential in the private market by providing high quality service and cuisine, maximizing their location and updating accommodation to a luxurious standard. There are many hotels which are primarily business-orientated during the week and open their doors to the lucrative wedding market at the weekend, but unfortunately still remain somewhat unimaginative in their décor, cuisine and accommodation. However, if they are keen for the weekend business a wedding brings them, they will be open to negotiating rates for both the catering costs and accommodation tariff and therefore are often very good value.

Sample menus

Many of these hotels offer wedding packages for couples and will supply sample wedding menus (see below) for your perusal. However, these are given purely as a guideline to help inspire and excite your taste buds and are not so regimented that they are unable to be changed.

(Crowne Plaza Reading – Berkshire)

A four course Wedding Breakfast

Canapés
***
Crown of Sweet Melon
filled with tropical fruits and drizzled with schnapps
Scottish Smoked Salmon
served with prawns and served with a lime crème fraiche
Breaded Rapid Fried Brie
with Drambuie syrup and fresh strawberries
Smoked Chicken and Parmesan Risotto
served with beetroot crisps
***
Soup or Sorbet course
Choose from our extensive selection
***
Roast Sirloin of Beef
served with Yorkshire pudding and roast gravy
Roast Lamb
with cranberry and mint stuffing and redcurrant jus
Roasted Entrecote of Pork
with a sweet calvados sauce
Confit Leg of Duck
served with an apricot and Grand Marnier jus
Poached Fillet of Sole
with asparagus and flavoured with Vermouth
Breast of Corn-Fed Chicken
served with wild mushrooms
***
Vanilla Cream Profiteroles
served with a warm chocolate and rum sauce
Lemon Tart
served with a sharp berry coulis
Tiramisu
with a vanilla sauce
Milk Chocolate Delice
with a duo of fruit coulis
***
Filter coffee or tea with Petit Fours

Top tip

Roman Maier, the executive sous chef of the Landmark Hotel, Marylebone, London says: 'A good chef is able to guarantee that the food the client sees and tastes at the menu tasting is the same on the actual wedding day by taking photographs and extensive notes.' He advises:

- Caterers should always try to use seasonal produce.
- Keep the food choice simple, as you are trying to please a wide choice of tastes.
- Consider choosing a buffet for one of the courses; a main course buffet or dessert buffet works well as it allows guests to mingle and socialize and stretch their legs!
- Choose a well-balanced menu without any duplication of ingredients.
- Think about the colour on the plate and how the food will be presented – your eye will taste the dish well before your palette.

Wedding packages

Many hotels and venues will offer wedding packages and often these are very good value and will incorporate many of the items you will need. However, if some items are superfluous and you feel that you would like to organize your own personal versions, there is often room for negotiation and management are usually happy to redesign the package.

Sample wedding package

(Crowne Plaza, Reading, Berkshire)

Red carpet on arrival: This is useful, and saves an additional expense.

Cake stand and bridal knife: Check that the cake stand is suitable for the style of cake you have ordered; for example, if your cake is square, make sure that there is a square version available.

Complimentary suite for bride and groom: This saves an extra cost and if you are leaving for honeymoon on the same night, you may be able to give this room to one set of parents.

Champagne in bride and groom's room: Most hotels will offer this to a couple, although not all.

Dedicated host: Having a member of the hotel's staff at the event is crucial, as they will be able to liaise between the best man, the catering staff and yourselves, and also save on booking a Master of Ceremonies. Check that they are aware of the timing for the day and all the details you have discussed in the run up to the wedding, particularly whether they will be making announcements on the day.

Room hire: This is a charge that is sometimes levied on top of the catering and can be substantial, depending on the venue.

Changing room for family: Being able to leave personal items and clothing in a room that is dedicated to your wedding is very useful. If you have a make-up artist/hairdresser coming to the venue before the ceremony, you will be able to use this room for the preparations. If you have children at the party, or elderly relatives, a private room can be very helpful later on in the evening for naps or quiet time away from the noise and excitement.

Flower arrangement for each table: Whether you decide to take up this option depends on your arrangements with your florist and how elaborate or specifio you are with the decorations. There is an obvious financial benefit of having flowers included in the package, however, always check on the style of arrangement and the colour scheme, which can usually be tailored to your requirements. Discuss with the hotel florist exactly what you will be given in the package cost and if you are not satisfied with the look, you may be able to discuss other ways of using the allocated budget so that the flowers blend well into your scheme. Alternatively, you may be able to put the cost of the flowers towards your own arrangements.

Table plan: A table plan designed by a hotel is usually done by computer and will be of a standard design. This is perfectly adequate unless you would like to opt for a more original version – in which case you may decline the offer.

Personalized menus: Each hotel will design its menus in a different way, and even if they are quite basic you may be able to jazz them up and personalize them to save on your printing costs. Ask to see some samples before making your final decision.

Place cards: Place cards are often printed on plain white card, which can be placed in your own holders, or used in your design for the table and so are another job you do not have to worry about.

Coloured balloons: Balloons can fill a room and transform a bland space into a colourful party scene. Once again, if you do not want to use them, perhaps you could choose to use the cost elsewhere.

Floating candles: This is a good idea for the tables and will add warmth and interest to them. You may have designed your own candle arrangements, but you can never have too many: I would always use these somewhere, even at the entrance or perhaps where the drinks reception is taking place or outside for an evening reception.

Disposable cameras: These can be quite costly to buy and therefore if the package includes them, it is a bonus!

Guest signature book: Some couples will have chosen a matching range of stationery for the whole occasion, including a guest book: but if you have not chosen this additional item, it may be useful.

Dinner in the restaurant prior to the wedding: Hotels who are sufficiently forward-thinking to understand the value of pleasing their clients and providing that extra something that their competitors do not offer, should be rewarded with business; it is these small gestures that will sway a couple who may be undecided about two similar venues for their wedding. What a lovely way to celebrate your forthcoming wedding than to take a couple of friends or family to the venue for dinner, or perhaps treat both parents to a pre-wedding meal!

Drinks

Supplying your own drinks

When discussing your choice of drinks, including alcohol and soft drinks, you should check whether it is possible to purchase your own beer, wine and spirits and if so, what corkage charge there will be. Sometimes it is a less expensive option to arrange for the alcohol to be bought in and pay any surcharge; however, costs should be carefully worked out, as often the caterer/venue is able to offer reasonable deals.

Budgeting

It is usual for couples to decide on a budget for drinks, particularly after the meal when there is often a cash or account bar set up. It is a common dilemma whether to ask guests to pay for their own drinks or not; realistically, if there is an open bar, it can become extremely expensive and you may be presented with a huge bill at the end of the night! Often hotels will offer a 'Drinks Package', which is a useful guideline as it allows you to budget for your alcohol expenditure, which is a large proportion of the overall expense. The following shows you the average amount of alcohol consumed at a wedding. However, each function is different and the final bill will reflect the number of guests you have invited and whether they are heavy drinkers! Average drinks consumption:

- 1 glass of champagne on arrival
- 2 glasses of wine with the meal
- 1 glass of champagne for the toast
- Liqueur/brandy with coffee.

It is advisable to agree a set drinks budget with the management: once that amount is reached ask to be informed, at which time you will be able to decide whether you want to increase the budget or change to a cash bar. This latter option is often the most popular choice as it allows the first few hours to be complimentary to guests as a courteous gesture; subsequently, it becomes a cash bar, when guests are very willing to pay for themselves as they realize that a free bar could become prohibitively expensive.

Chic cocktails

Cocktails served in funky coloured glasses are very popular and can be served instead of, or as well as, champagne at the reception. A signature cocktail can add a really exclusive touch to your wedding. You could have a cocktail each created to suit both your personalities and serve them at the reception.

As the trend for cocktails at weddings has increased, so have the companies offering this service. Create Cocktails are experts in the art of 'mixology' – creating contemporary, trendy cocktails guaranteed to 'shake things up' a little. They say: 'Imagine your guests' delight at watching a line up of talented barmen mixing, shaking and pouring delicious concoctions of specially designed cocktails to complement your menu.' The choice is yours: you many only want a basic bar area at the wedding with staff to serve your drinks, or you may choose to book a funky mobile bar complete with exciting theatrical displays from 'flair' barmen.

Bar hire

A new concept in serving drinks at weddings is hiring a bespoke bar that can be designed to your specification and erected in the marquee, hotel or venue booked, to add style and efficiency to what is usually a very mundane part of the catering services. Bash Bars suggest: 'You should consider a range of facilities when ordering a bar for your wedding, from back bars, display coolers and fantastic-looking bar furniture for hire. You may even want to choose a bar which incorporates the latest LED light change technology, enabling a range of lighting effects at the press of a button. Start the evening with a blue bar and end it with red, green or purple – the choice is yours!' These bars have a funky, space-age design, which blend beautifully with a contemporary space, but also work very well in a more traditional environment – such as a stately home – as they combine the old and the new in a modern, fun way. Graphics to co-ordinate with the theme could be designed and the imagery custom-made and displayed as a backdrop. Why not have a circular bar lit with funky, neon lighting with waiters entertaining guests while mixing and shaking your favourite combinations, recreating a scene from the Tom Cruise film *Cocktail*!

The wedding cake

Occasionally the caterer will offer to supply the wedding cake, but more often than not the couple choose to use an independent cake maker. You may have a relative who has offered to make the cake, which can save a great deal of money; however, you will need to be happy with the result and if you have any doubts, perhaps you could ask them to bake some individual cookies iced with guest's names to use as place cards, instead of having the responsibility of the creating the culinary centrepiece of the day!

Wild and wacky designs

There are some incredible designs available: everything from individual fairy cakes, iced with the words 'Marry me', 'I love you', 'Hitched' and so on, arranged on tiered glass cake stands, to 5ft-high decadently wicked chocolate fudge cakes, covered in Belgium white chocolate and decorated with ornate cherubs cascading down the layers! Wedding cakes have become another way of expressing your own personalities. You may want to represent a particular interest or hobby you share as a couple, or recreate a significant event in your lives: such as using turtles and sea life to adorn an aqua green creation, perhaps, if you met while deep sea diving!

Hand-painted cakes to match pretty vintage china teacups for an old fashioned look and tiers of passion fruit, carrot and lemon cakes have taken the place of the traditional rich fruit cake, offering a fresher, tastier option for the modern bride and groom.

The *croquembouche* is often requested: a pyramid of choux buns, filled with fresh cream or crème patisserie, covered in spun sugar and chocolate – it is a truly wonderfully theatrical choice, but a horror to cut into, so let the experts do it behind the scenes.

Cake stands

Individual cup cakes, or fairy cakes arranged on a perspex or glass-tiered cake stand create a stunning display and each cake can be individually decorated to your colour scheme and theme. The tiered cake stands are available to hire or buy from catering equipment hire firms in a variety of styles and shapes, such as heart, petal, square and circle design. An average stand can hold up to 140 cakes as a seven-tier display, but this can be added to in order to create an amazing 20-tier skyscraper! Stands are available in a huge variety of shapes from three-tiered swans, 'S' shapes, 'C' shapes, step stands and so on.

Wedding cake tops

A mini replica of the bride and groom made from icing or even plastic used to be seen regularly on the top of wedding cakes. Today, if couples are having a novelty cake with a humorous twist, then cake makers are still asked to produce look-a-likes, but it is done very much tongue-in-cheek! Fresh flowers or sugared creations are the most popular; however, there are endless designs available to the modern couple! Innovative designers realize that you are keen to find more and more unique suppliers offering services that are new and exciting. The possibility of adorning the top of your wedding cake with a handcrafted, personalized sculpture, made from stunning raw silk, as a miniature version of the couple is a very exciting and new concept. Designer Kathy Scott says: 'A bride often wants a cake top that she can keep and with this version, every aspect of the wedding couple is scrutinized to recreate every minute detail: starting with sketches of the dress and the groom's outfit. The artwork is presented in an elegant glass case as an everlasting memento and a wonderful heirloom for generations to come. Today, couples are seeking out truly inspirational ideas for each and every detail of their wedding and want to make their wedding as personal and individual as possible.'

Cutting of the cake

The cutting of the cake is ceremonial, with the bride placing her hand over the groom's while they both cut into the lower tier with a silver knife; once cut, it usually prompts a spontaneous round of applause from their guests! Traditionally, the top tier – which was always rich fruit cake – would be taken away and given to the couple to keep as the christening cake for their firstborn child. As fruit cake is no longer the preferred choice, this tradition has generally faded away and the cake is cut up by staff and distributed with coffee after the meal, or sometimes placed on a buffet table to enjoy later on in the evening.

Visiting wedding cake makers

Some cake makers specialize in cutting-edge designs and will have websites with photographs of their cakes. However, like many other aspects of the arrangements, a personal visit to the supplier – to sample the taste of the cake and to take a first-hand look at their spectacular creations – is a must. Although time-consuming, it is always beneficial in the long run to spend a while getting to know your suppliers and building a relationship with them, as they will then be able to offer a more personal service and you will feel more assured. There are a few cake makers renowned for creating wonderful wedding cakes in unusual mediums. Designs featuring a conical shape wrapped from top to bottom in edible sugar parchment, or covered in mini cones of sugar parchment which can be dusted to your colour scheme, and towers of dark, white and milk chocolate chards dominate the showrooms. Options such as dessert cakes, with mini summer puddings, fancies and parcels of individually-wrapped cake are very cost effective as they double-up both as the gorgeous centrepiece for the wedding photographs as well as replacing a dessert on the menu, therefore saving money.

Top tip

Specialist cake maker Linda Fripp says: 'If the budget is tight, or if the number of guests is smaller than the size that a dramatic cake caters for, ask for the base of the cake to be real – so that when you cut into it, you are able to cut a slice – whereas the remainder of the cake could be fake, but covered in authentic decoration to give the illusion of a complete masterpiece! This way, the costs are kept to a minimum as the cake is whisked away for cutting, and behind-the-scenes staff have been provided with a pre-prepared cutting cake in the desired flavour to give to your guests.'

Chocolate fountains

As an alternative to the wedding cake – or perhaps as an alternative to a dessert – a chocolate fountain, using Belgian dark, milk or white chocolate, has become a new and exciting addition to the proceedings! The spectacle, taste and aroma of warm chocolate cascading down the fountain will keep your guests entertained and talking long after the day. These are extremely popular for weddings now, and fountains can be hired from numerous outlets, some with displays on fabulous perspex bases lit with multi-coloured neon to suit your theme. This centrepiece comes into its own in the evening, when the lights are dimmed. Guests can help themselves to a delight of scrumptious dipping foods arranged in chequerboards on the clear perspex and in funky-coloured glass bowls. Foods such as: fresh strawberries, pineapple and kiwi, decadently delicious flapjacks, almond and pistachio nougat, heart-shaped marshmallows, brownies and meringues or homemade Cornish fudge in mouth-watering flavours. White chocolate is often chosen for the fountain as it resembles the look of a wedding cake; however, it is possible to create the most tempting combinations of chocolate to satisfy your every whim, for example chocolate orange, strawberry chocolate, mint chocolate – the list is endless!

Champagne/wine fountains

Fifties film star Jayne Mansfield had such a passion for pink that she had a fountain of rose champagne installed in her Hollywood mansion. Like fashion, weddings are influenced by society and current trends, which is why a fun option such as wine or champagne fountains are proving to be a hit; everyone wants a more glamorous lifestyle and a wedding is an ideal opportunity to indulge in your fantasies and enjoy every element of the party. Glasses are filled from a continuous flowing fountain of wine or champagne, and you and your guests can fill your glasses all night long in a fun and stylish way. These devices can be hired if you are organizing your own party and uniformed staff accompany the fountain to keep it topped up and to maintain the replacement of the glasses.

Chocolates and after dinner novelties

Why not serve coffee with after dinner chocolates wrapped in a romantic message. Directors Fiona Cox and Lizzie Thornton-Allan of Cox and Cox say: 'Couples are interested in sourcing gorgeous, unique items to dress their tables and want the choice of a wide range of fun items, such as surprise balls made from crêpe paper, which are a sophisticated version of pass the parcel. Pass them around the table after the meal and your guests will have great fun un-wrapping each layer to reveal a small charm gift – a lot less fattening than chocolates!'

How about an origami fortune-teller – a fabulously original little extra for your wedding which will also be considered a quirky keepsake of a memorable day? Ask someone close to you to choose a coloured heart, lift the flap and read them the romantic French phrase underneath.

Continuing an oriental theme, fortune sticks are an ancient form of Chinese fortune-telling and each one is inscribed with an individual fate. When tucked inside napkins or as unusual place setting markers, your guests will be intrigued and entertained.

Wedding matches are a useful addition to the table, to be used for lighting candles and for guests to take away. These can be printed with dictionary definitions of wedlock and include the words 'The Perfect Match'.

Crackers can be pulled at weddings as well as Christmas, perhaps made in white with each containing a snap, romantic quotation and a silver plated charm, giving your guests a reason to turn to one another and introduce themselves as they pull their crackers and break the ice at the same time!

Decorative brown sugar hearts perched on the side of a coffee cup would make a delicious drink even more special, or fill a glass bowl with decorative sugar cubes with pink and red hearts on them; an extravagance indeed, but one that will be truly appreciated by your friends and family as they sweeten their coffee or tea after the meal!

09 the flowers

In this chapter you will learn:

- **top tips for flower arrangements**
- **what to consider when choosing a florist**
- **suggestions for bridal bouquets**
- **about flowers for the bridal party including bridesmaids' flowers and headdresses**
- **the meaning of flowers**
- **how to preserve your bouquet**
- **about seasonal flowers**
- **about various confetti options.**

Choosing your florist

The emphasis with wedding flowers is now fun, relaxed and informal! Brides want innovative, creative flowers using artistic arrangements and quirky containers to capture the essence of the day.

Top tip

Expert florist, Mary Jane Vaughan suggests: 'If brides are limited in their budgets, always choose one or two stunning arrangements with the wow factor, rather than lots of smaller, less exciting displays which will only disappear into the background. At the reception, do not spend your entire budget on the flowers at the entrance, as guests will see these as they arrive and not enjoy them again until they go home, at which time, they will probably not notice them at all. Instead concentrate on the tables, where guests will be spending the majority of their time and make them particularly special, in whichever way you are theming the wedding, so that they are a talking point. If possible pin spot them, so that the flowers become the focal point of the decoration and add scent, beauty and excitement to the event. Roses or lilies are beautiful flowers, but if your budget is limited, opt for less expensive, but equally beautiful blooms such as gerbera and freesia.'

Before venturing out to find the perfect florist, it is advisable to look through specialist flower magazines, such as *Wedding Flowers*, which show a vast array of designs and give advice on all aspects of wedding flowers. You will then be armed with the knowledge you need to visit several of your local florists, with your ideas and thoughts for colours and favourite blooms. Perhaps family and friends may have used a shop or individual they are happy to recommend, which would be a useful starting point. Begin the decision process by looking through their portfolio of wedding bouquets, church, ceremony and reception flowers.

What to look out for

It is always more reassuring to see actual photographs of the work a florist has done and the reception venues they have decorated with their arrangements, rather than simply looking at an album of cuttings from other florists and magazines, which they assure you they can replicate. They may very well be able to recreate these complicated designs; however, you only have their word and will have a better guarantee of the finished product if you find a florist who is experienced and has taken the time to record their work in a professional manner. Hopefully the personality of the florist will help you to form an opinion quite quickly as to whether you would like your flowers to be designed by them, as you will need to be confident that they will produce exactly what you have in mind. They should be able to advise and guide you and be happy to spend time chatting through your ideas and queries.

Discussing your ideas

You can then begin to discuss in detail the flowers you would like, depending on your budget. Take note of the shop's style which is a good indication to the quality and service you will receive. Sometimes the florist will even make up a mock version of the bouquet and table centrepiece for your approval, which is hugely beneficial as it allows you to see exactly what you will be presented with on the day, and any changes can be discussed and agreed prior to final payment.

Costs

Always clarify the final amount in writing, so that there are no hidden extras added to the bill at a later stage, such as delivery, wire or ribbon costs. Finally, the date of your wedding could be at one of the busiest and most expensive times of the year for flowers, such as Valentine's Day, Mother's Day or Christmas, so be aware of the potential increase in costs.

Bridal bouquets

Hand-tied bouquets are the most popular style chosen by modern brides, and whatever your preferences, there are a huge variety available. For a rich stunning bouquet, why not choose a posy of Scarlet Red, Julia and Terracotta roses and privet berries, tied with matching organza ribbon. A bouquet hand-tied with taffeta ribbon and bursting with cream Nova Zembia and White Lydia roses may suit an ivory theme. A very simple bouquet may be made with sweet peas, hyacinths, tulips and philodendron leaves, with the stems bound with satin ribbon and studded with pearl pins.

Some brides do not want an elaborate bouquet or even a small posy, but opt instead to carry a single bloom, such as a calla lily, a shower arrangement of orchids, or even a trailing wrist corsage. Remember that hand-tied posies consisting of flowers in season at the time of the wedding work out much more reasonable than an elaborate, individually-wired bouquet of exotic blooms that need to be imported; if the budget is tight, make sure that the florist has suggested various ways of cutting costs.

Colours

Discuss the colours of your bouquet with your florist and whether they will complement your skin colouring, as often a paler bride may need a brighter colour to warm her tones and prevent her from looking washed-out.

Flowers for the bridal party

Bridesmaids' flowers

Bear in the mind the age of the child/children before you make a decision on the flowers for them. Very small children may be happy to hold a small posy; however, older ones may be able to manage a decorated basket filled with fresh, silk or paper rose petals or bougainvillea and would enjoy the important job of scattering them down the aisle, before the bride makes her entrance.

Top tip

Be careful if using fresh rose petals to scatter on a light coloured carpet, as they main stain the fabric when trodden on!

Bridesmaids' headdresses

Headdresses for young children should be carefully thought about; they may be tempted to fiddle and play with a fresh flower headdress during a long church service or civil ceremony, and therefore it may not look its best for the photographs afterwards! If you have older bridesmaids looking after the little ones, they should be able to supervise, otherwise consider having a headdress made from artificial flowers that cannot be so easily damaged, and which can be kept as a memento to use for parties or dressing-up following the wedding.

Groom

Traditionally the groom wears a buttonhole made up of two flowers in his left lapel, which tends to match one of the flowers featured in his bride's bouquet.

Best man and fathers of the bride/groom

The best man and fathers of the bride/groom also wear a buttonhole with two flowers in their left lapel, which is different from the groom, but should co-ordinate with the theme.

Mother of the bride/groom

Both mothers traditionally wear a corsage that may complement their outfits, which in turn usually blend in with the whole colour scheme. These can be worn on the ensemble, or around the mothers' wrists.

Ushers

The ushers should wear a single buttonhole in their left lapel to match the bridal party. These are usually less ornate than those of the groom, best man and fathers.

Pageboy

If the pageboy is to wear a buttonhole it should match the best man's arrangement.

The meanings of flowers

Here are some of the most popular bridal blooms and their meanings.

Flower	Meaning
Acacia	Friendship
Alyssum	Incomparable worth
Amaryllis	Pride, beauty
Anemone	Forsaken
Bluebell	Humility
Buttercup	Riches, childishness

Flower	Meaning
Carnation (pink)	I'll never forget you
Carnation (red)	My heart aches for you
Daisy	Innocent
Heather	Admiration
Hydrangea	Thank you for understanding
Ivy	Wedded love, fidelity, friendship
Lavender	Devotion, caution
Lily (tiger)	Wealth, pride
Lily (white)	Purity, virginity
Lily of valley	Increased happiness
Lotus flower	Sweetness, rejected love
Mistletoe	Affection
Moss	Charity, maternal love
Narcissus	Egotism
Orchid	Love, beauty
Pansy	Thoughts, consideration
Peony	Happy life
Rose (bridal)	Happy love
Rose (dark pink)	Thank you
Rose (peach)	Enthusiasm, desire
Rose (pink)	Perfect, you're lovely
Rose (red)	I love you
Rose (white)	Youth
Rose (tea)	I'll remember always
Stock	Lasting love
Stephanotis	Happiness in marriage
Sweet pea	Goodbye – blissful pleasure
Thyme	Activity
Tulip (red)	Believe in me
Tulip (variegated)	Beautiful eyes
Tulip (yellow)	Hopeless love
Veronica	Fidelity
Violet (purple)	Faithfulness
Violet (white)	Let's take a chance
White rose bud	Awakening love

Reception flowers

Once your scheme has been chosen, perhaps inspired by a favourite flower, colour or scent, the venue can be enhanced and transformed with original designs that will reflect your personalities and style. If the venue is a traditionally ornate stately home, with an eclectic mix of colour, furnishings and fabrics, elegant arrangements of white and cream flowers and soft green foliage will not overpower and compete with the décor; if it is a more contemporary hotel, perhaps some trendy, modern designs would complement and enhance the space. A marquee can often seem very bare, however its neutrality could also been used to your advantage and act as a blank canvas on which to stamp your own individual style – and provide you and your florist with a challenge to bring the stark whiteness of the interior to life by injecting some bold statements of colour and shape!

Top tip

If you are organizing the flowers yourself, try not to design a floral centrepiece for the tables that is too tall and full – unless it is a candelabra with a thin stem and with the bulk of the flowers above your guests' heads. Otherwise your guests will not be able to see each other and will spend all their time trying to look either side of the flowers to talk to the person opposite!

Gifts for the mother of the bride/groom

At the end of the speeches it has been traditional to present both mothers with a bouquet or posy of flowers to thank them for all their hard work, which your florist will be able to supply. Modern couples tend to choose a more personal gift to give to their mothers, as flowers will not have the lasting pleasure of a well thought out present, which they can keep as a reminder of the day.

Wedding cake flowers

Cakes are often decorated with flowers featured in the bride's bouquet or in the table arrangements.

Throwing the bouquet

The custom of tossing the bouquet has its roots in England. It was considered that the bride brought good fortune to others – in order to do this, spectators would try to obtain some of her clothing and flowers by ripping them off her! In a bid to escape, the bride would throw her bouquet to the crowd and it was said that the single woman who caught it was the one who received all her good fortune and therefore would be next to marry. Sometimes today's brides want to keep their bouquet and so will arrange for the florist to make up some smaller posies to toss to their single friends!

Bouquet preservation

If the bride has decided to keep her bouquet and have it professionally preserved, it is very important to make sure that it is kept in a cool place until it can be delivered to, or collected by the relevant company, as they will need to have it in the best possible condition in order to optimize the quality of the final product. Bouquets and posies can be freeze-dried and displayed in 3-D picture frames, Victorian-style domed acrylic and glass cases, or more modern versions in chic glass cubes. Individual flowers and petals can also be encased in glass paperweights which make ideal presents for family members after the wedding and will be special mementos of the day for years to come. You may choose to have a painting commissioned by an artist who will recreate one or two of the blooms from your bouquet onto a stretched canvas for a contemporary keepsake for your new home, or enlarged photographs can be printed onto canvas and made into a stylish piece of artwork.

Ideas for fun flower arrangements

- Topiary trees standing either side of the entrance look fabulous covered loosely with tulle and tied with a co-ordinating ribbon and can be lit at night with fairy lights.
- Mini terracotta pots filled with herbs, tied with a gingham ribbon and placed on each table add scent and a rustic element to the venue.
- Galvanized pots hung on the end of the pews and filled with sweet peas are an inexpensive way of bringing a natural style to the ceremony decoration.

- Twigs sprayed with white and sparkling with glitter would be perfect for a winter wedding and ornaments could be hung on the branches.
- Large glass fish bowls on each table filled with an orchid or two wrapped around the inside is a stunningly simple but effective choice – perfect for a contemporary wedding.
- Grouping on the table works very well. By creating varying heights you will achieve an interesting display, for example using a mirror as a base with different lengths and sizes of candles.
- Centrepieces decorated with butterflies suspended in the air, as though flying around the table, or soft multicoloured feathers add drama and texture.
- Mini pots of pale pink hydrangeas make gorgeous table centrepieces.
- Delicate sprigs of pink lilac arrangements displayed in tall cream vases produce a wonderfully light scent as well as adding a natural romantic look.
- Hydrangeas in water then placed in decorative gift bags make a unique table display.

Flowers on a budget

Using foliage is a great way of bulking out your displays and saving money at the same time. Ivy comes in many shades: variegated, dark green and rich russets can all be found in local gardens, making it a wonderfully inexpensive and versatile addition to your decoration. It can be used in many ways: tied loosely to wrap napkins, draped around seating plans to add interest, or intertwined down a staircase balustrade to create a stunning effect, especially when paired with twinkling fairy lights. Eucalyptus is another fantastic variety of foliage which when used in boughs can be linked between chairs for a civil ceremony and placed on the floor following the run of an aisle carpet to enhance the walkway.

Seasonal flowers

Flower	Colour/appearance
SPRING	
Genista	creamy white, yellow branches of small flowers
Hyacinth	violet, blue, crimson, pink, white, cream spikes of tubular flowers that often have a strong scent
Lilac	white or mauve tiny, star-shaped flowers on tall, woody stems
Sweet pea	pink, cream and mauve long displays of pretty frilled flowers
SUMMER	
Ammi	white large umbrella head made up of lots of tiny flowers
Delphinium	blue, purple, white towering spikes of flowers
Hydrangea	white, pink, blue, lilac, green, red/brown star-shaped flowers in wide flower heads
Peony	white, pale or deep pink, pale peach, maroon beautiful, big flower heads
Sweet William	very colourful, variegated petals in a variety of shades with lots of tiny flowers which form a dense head
AUTUMN	
Hellebore	white purple, cream, green, pink saucer-shaped flowers that grow in clusters
Hypericum	yellow flowers and berries in red, orange and brown cup-shaped flowers
Nerine	hot or pale pink open sprays of slender petals curled like ribbons
Sedum	shades of pinky-brown, with light green stems, clusters of star shaped flowers
Zinnia	bright yellow, red or orange, often with black stripes on each petal, large flat-headed blooms

Flower	Colour/appearance
WINTER	
Amaryllis	from white and pale pink to bright crimson and deep burgundy, huge, open trumpet shape
Anemone	red, purple, pink or white with a black centre and large, flat flower head
Mimosa	yellow tiny clusters of balls on woody stems
Paperwhite	pure white delicate and pretty star-shaped blooms
Ranunculus	white, yellow, orange, red, pink bowl-shaped heads
YEAR ROUND	
Beargrass	green, very long and slender pointed grass
Carnation	a broad range of colours with large flower heads
Eucalyptus	green, silver-green or blue-green foliage, round or long leaves
Freesia	lilac, pink, white, a tiny, strongly-scented delicate flower
Gerbera	many wild colours in large, daisy-like blooms
Lisianthus	purple, cream, pink, or pale green, plus two-toned varieties with quite small, very delicate bell-shaped flowers
Long Lily	pure white with long yellow centre, trumpet-shaped flower head
Orchid	white exotic flowers, ranging from small Singapore orchids to larger bolder versions
Rose	a huge range of shades and variety of sizes available
Ruscus	dark green foliage with oval or pointed leaves
Tulip	a multitude of colours, trumpet-shaped flowers

Confetti

Food was always a popular choice to be thrown at married couples as it symbolized plentiful crops! The word 'confetti' is thought to have derived from the Italian root word for 'confectionery' as sweets and sugar-coated nuts were thrown at Italian couples! Historically the English threw rice in the hope that they would be successful and prosperous and have many children to work on the land; and in Morocco figs, dates and raisins were used to encourage a fruitful union.

Today couples have realized that rice is not such a great idea, especially as it is quite painful if you are caught in the eye with a few grains, or if they manage to land down the front of your dress, they are very difficult to retrieve! The alternative of using fresh or freeze-dried rose petals and other flowers such as bougainvillea – available through mail order companies such as Passion for Petals – is a much more pleasant option. They are supplied in a wide range of colours from pinks, burgundys and lilacs to champagne gold and ivory white, to suit any scheme. The bougainvillea – which is grown in the tropics and sent to the UK by boat – provides a small industry in West Africa with employment. It is a wonderfully light, thin petal that floats beautifully as confetti and has tropical connotations, whereas the rose, associated with romance and hundreds of years of history from Cleopatra to today, is always a favourite with brides.

Handmade paper confetti cones can be used to hold the petals and are an attractive and stylish addition to the day; they can be displayed in baskets for the flower girls/bridesmaids to distribute to guests after the ceremony. Even the cones themselves are available in some beautifully creative papers, such as spun sugar cones – the modern day equivalent of the sugar cones given as love tokens in medieval England. They are not made of sugar, but resemble spun sugar, and can be filled with petals, or even edible goodies such as sugared almonds to offer to your guests. Alternative papers could be textured mulberry paper, parchment, or even newspaper, or music sheets for a themed wedding.

Car flowers

If you are using a transport company to provide a car to take you to the church/ceremony/venue, check with them if they supply a floral decoration for the interior; if so, will it be fresh and will it co-ordinate with your scheme? Your florist will be able to liaise with them and provide a suitable arrangement. Most car companies do have flowers in their cars; however, they can be made of plastic in gaudy colours and very dusty – so beware!

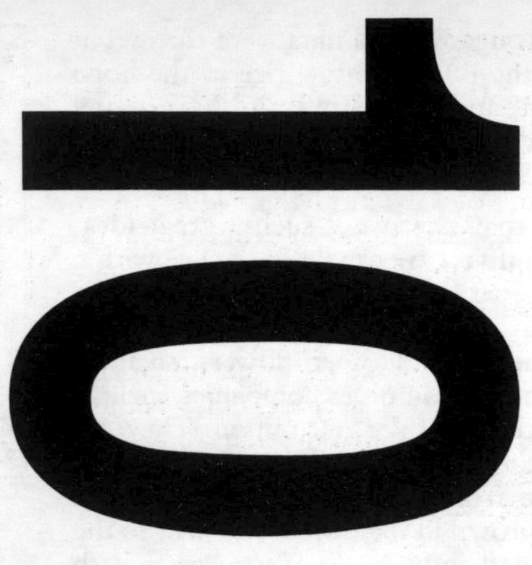

photographs/video

In this chapter you will learn:

- **how to choose a good photographer**
- **questions to ask**
- **timings and scheduling**
- **about changes in modern photography**
- **about styles of presentation**
- **about videos/filming.**

Choosing a photographer

Photographs are the only tangible reminder you will have after the wedding day has passed and therefore they must rank at the top of your priority list (together with the venue). Sourcing a good photographer has become easier with the introduction of advertising through websites, as many show an extensive range of their work online, which you can peruse prior to a meeting. However, it has also opened the doors to many more inexperienced photographers who have the potential to post glossy photographs on their sites without the back up of the experience that is necessary to execute a successful wedding shoot. On the positive side, it has eliminated the time and effort involved in arranging meetings with a selection of photographers to look through their albums and portfolios; today couples can sit at home or work and look through a potential photographer's work on the internet at their leisure, before seeing them in person to ascertain if the photographer's personality and style of work is compatible with their own personal expectations.

Top tip

Always check that the portfolio you are looking through is the work of the actual photographer you intend to book. Occasionally a photographer will belong to a group or a company which display each others' work, either on the website or in person. It is vital that you ask to see their own personal portfolios, otherwise you may be disappointed as each photographer has their own style.

Dress code

Discuss the dress code for the day. For example, if the wedding is black tie, the photographer should also be in appropriate attire, so that they blend in with your guests; likewise if lounge suits are the order of the day, they should be asked to wear a suitable outfit, so that they do not turn up in jeans and a t-shirt (unless of course, your wedding is a very casual affair, and you have agreed a 'look' prior to the day).

Things to check

Do they have an assistant?

Nowadays many photographers have assistants, or partners they work with, so that all angles of the proceedings are covered – literally! You may find that one of their team is waiting at the church or the ceremony venue to capture guests arriving, while the other photographer is at the house following the bride and her party with their preparations. This enables them both to take advantage of any memorable shots that might happen before the marriage. Having an extra photographer is extremely useful as no photographic opportunity is missed.

How long will they be staying?

Check with your photographer how long he/she will be staying. It used to be that only certain key aspects of the day were covered: for example, the ceremony, drinks reception, and a mock-up of the cutting of the cake; then the photographer would disappear even before the wedding breakfast began! Thankfully this has changed and photographers are more willing to stay for the majority of the day, and will photograph your final exit from the celebrations as well to complete the story.

Will they cover any special aspects of the day?

This is a good idea if you have arranged for a particular form of transport – a sports car, helicopter or maybe a hot air balloon – to whisk you away to your first night hotel or honeymoon destination; when you have spent a great deal of time, effort and money organizing a particular aspect of the wedding, it is always a great shame if you do not have a record of it.

Will they photograph all the personal images?

This is why it is important to learn from a portfolio if he/she is the kind of photographer who likes to include personal images, such as the embroidery on the wedding gown, the bride's shoes, a stunning veil, or headdress. All these small, but very important features of the whole wedding have been thought about very carefully and designed to the last detail and it is wonderful to have close-up images of the results of all your hard work for you both to cherish and remember.

Do they know the schedule for the day?

It is vital that your photographer has a copy of your schedule/itinerary for the day. If you have a Wedding Planner, he/she will liaise with all suppliers to confirm the running order of the day. If not, it is wise to make sure that everyone knows what the schedule is, to avoid any misunderstandings.

Will they visit the venue before the wedding?

Most photographers, if unfamiliar with the venue you have chosen, will suggest that they arrange a meeting with you on site so that they can familiarize themselves with the layout, rooms and outside areas, making note of any key backdrops and interesting features that may be suitable to highlight on the day.

Are they aware of any personal issues with family/friends?

It is at this meeting that you will have an ideal opportunity to air any queries you may have and bring up any issues within your family, for example any contentious issues with divorced or separated parents that may cause friction on the day. The photographer will welcome any information you can give to save embarrassment to yourselves and your family.

Have they met or discussed the day with venue management?

You should also liaise with the venue management to confirm that there are no problems you need to be aware of before the day, for example 'out-of-bounds' areas. They will be able to suggest a suitable space for photographs should the weather change and your first choice is not feasible.

New styles in wedding photography

Wedding photography has changed dramatically in the past five to ten years. The traditional wedding photographer offered standard, quite structured services with set prices, packages and albums, sometimes lacking in creativity and inspiration! Couples were left with formal set-ups at the wedding – generally in colour only – which did not suit the majority; couples were often hesitant and felt awkward with a photographer who needed his subjects to pose stiffly and unnaturally. Wedding photographers were also seen in a bad light, due to their strict regime on the day and the lack of spontaneity. There were often delays getting to the reception, as lengthy poses were arranged outside the church and once again at the reception. Couples were often whisked off to a nearby location for shots which took them away from their guests and the party, sometimes delaying the running order of the day. Modern photographers have noticed the change in client's expectations.

Modern wedding photography

Reportage is a word that has become synonymous with modern wedding photography in recent years. The word is used liberally in wedding publications to describe any photography that looks informal and relaxed. In reality, true reportage is documentary-style photography, which means that there is no contact at all between the photographer and the subject. Events are taken exactly as they happen. As we all know, this is not usually the case at weddings. Often the photographer will have at least some contact with the couple and their guests, even if it's only during the formal photographs.

Posing for shots

Photographers are often asked for very natural shots and are requested that they do not ask couples to stand in awkward poses. However, because the photographer is asking the couple to do something, it doesn't mean that it will look stuffy. Modern photography is about doing quite the opposite! Couples should keep in mind that many of the candid and fun images they like in the magazines and on websites only 'look' natural because many modern wedding photographers have a gentle way of directing their brides and grooms to appear spontaneous and relaxed.

Contemporary wedding photographers will not just take pictures, but will look to tell the story of the day in images that will truly capture the mood and ambience of the whole wedding. This includes everything from the nervous preparations of the bride and groom, through to the emotion of the ceremony and joy at the reception, as well as sensory images, such as: a beautiful perfume bottle, exquisite flowers, handmade place cards, the arrangement of gifts, and stunning architecture. These images are just as important to set the scene and tell the couple's story in a fluid and imaginative style.

Fashion and glamour

Influenced by the popularity of celebrity magazine shoots, wedding photography has become much glossier! One trend that's catching on quickly in the UK is the 'fashion and glamour' style images of the bride and groom taken after the ceremony. Photographer Julia Boggio says: 'Artistically, I really enjoy this part of the wedding, where I whisk the bride and groom off for some alone time during the drinks reception. Couples always love these photographs when I show them, as these images capture how beautiful they felt on their wedding day.'

Post-production

A photographer's skill in post-production is also important. It's where skin is smoothed, blemishes are erased and colours are corrected and boosted. Sometimes, as Julia says: 'Image manipulation software helps me get rid of any imperfections that may have been unavoidable on the day. For example, a groom at one of my weddings had received a black eye a few days earlier, so I was able to lighten the skin and make it less noticeable. Another example is a bride whose underwear was accidentally showing in one shot; she was made to look perfectly respectable by enhanced imagery!'

Fees

One last consideration with wedding photography is cost. There are photographers who will fit any budget, but photography is one area where you get what you pay for. In five or ten years' time, it won't matter how much the photographs cost. What will matter are the beautiful memories of your wedding day.

Top tip

Photographer Julia Boggio suggests: 'A couple should always check that the photographer has a clear schedule for delivering the goods after the wedding. He or she should be able to inform you of exactly when the images will be ready for viewing and have a firm timeline in place for completion of the album (for example, six weeks from design approval).' Many photographers will arrange for you to come to their home or studio when you are back from honeymoon to view the images in a relaxed environment. All the images are often uploaded onto a dedicated website, with a password that guests can use to access the pictures and place orders for prints and albums. This advance in technology has enabled family and friends to enjoy the privilege of being able to look at the couple's complete wedding story and relive all those wonderful moments in a way that was not feasible before the joys of the internet.

List of shots

It is useful to let your photographer know in advance if you would like particular photographs taken of groups of people; he/she will ensure that they are not overlooked. For example, you may have a special relative who has travelled a great distance to be with you at the wedding and whom you do not see very often, therefore a group shot with all the members of your family would be an ideal keepsake for everyone. Perhaps you have an elderly relative at the wedding who means a great deal to you, or maybe it is the first time that all your girlfriends who are usually scattered around the country are together.

Presentation of the photographs

The final presentation of the photographs has recently become another area of wedding photography that is very exciting, with the introduction of new and stylish albums and wedding books! In the past, photographs have been chosen by the couple and mounted by hand in an album offered by the photographer, often made in a basic acrylic material, faux leather, or perhaps a genuine leather-bound design at the higher end of the market. There are still companies offering this service; however, the majority of photographers have discarded this rather old-fashioned approach in favour of a state-of-the-art alternative.

Graphistudio coffee table book

Italy has always been the leading manufacturer of high-quality presentation albums for photographs and within the past five or six years the introduction of the Graphistudio coffee table book, or limited edition story books, has revolutionized wedding photography. These books are incredibly beautiful and stylish, made from metallic photographic paper, onto which digital photographs are printed, a quality of finish that would be found in a glossy magazine or hard-backed publication.

Creative wedding photographers are also using this method of presentation. Dave Waller, photographer says: 'Couples are now seeking a stylish contemporary image. By using a variety of lens such as long, wide, and fish eye, a photographer is able to produce fabulously creative angles with exciting results and by presenting the photographs in an Italian wedding book, they have an incredible impact!' They are available in several sizes enabling the photographer to arrange a collage of scenes representing and telling the story of the day. These books really do have the 'wow factor' and are proudly displayed on coffee tables nationwide, for visiting friends and family to view and marvel at for many years.

Smaller versions of these books are also available, known as 'parent' (12 inch x 8 inch /A4) or 'pocket' books (6 inch x 4 inch). These are identical in content to the larger coffee table books, but are ideal to give to family and friends as gifts. A current trend is to use these as a gift to give to all the guests at the wedding, instead of favours; although a somewhat costlier substitute this would make a fabulous gift and would be treasured for years to come.

New exciting ways of presenting wedding photographs are coming onto the market all the time; one of the most unusual is a wedding print made into a rug or a tapestry, woven with coloured thread to create a replica of the bride or couple, to hang on the wall or use in the lounge as a carpet!

Videos

The trend for having a video of the wedding went through a decline as it was thought that many of the videographers were somewhat intrusive on the day and their styles too gimmicky.

Alan Howard of The Wedding Documentary Company believes: 'One of the reasons for the decline is because the term "Wedding Video" has been shorthand for a very boring, overly long, usually quite cheesy music montage of all the sloppy bits of the day.' This is a common consensus shared by many couples having watched their friends' lengthy wedding videos at some time or other. Alan adds: 'Actually the day has all the ingredients for a hugely entertaining TV documentary, with a guaranteed happy ending that leaves you feeling great. You could even include the background players in the film, such as the chef commenting on the food, the musicians expressing their joy at playing the music and the flower arrangers explaining the wonderful blooms that have been chosen, to produce a fantastic short film that is as good as anything on TV!'

Finding the right wedding video company

Thankfully this decline has now changed with the introduction of a new, more stylish documentary approach by companies offering professional film makers and cameramen with experience of producing and directing high quality films. Some creative and forward-thinking film makers have been at the forefront of helping to change the UK's perception of wedding video companies and are skilled in creative wedding cinematography: they produce a magical moving memory of your special day, edited to your favourite music tracks. Employing a company with a solid track record will give you a greater reassurance that they are able to provide a professional, polished service. However, MD Janet Fenton of The Graham Fenton Experience, a market leader, advises couples: 'The most important aspect of finding the right videographer to shoot your wedding is ensuring that they will offer a personal enthusiastic service and have the experience to know when and where to get the best footage without being in the way or at all intrusive on the day.' They may have impressive glossy literature or a fabulous website – and even all the up-to-date equipment – but if they do not care enough about the final product, you will not receive a film that reflects the true essence of the day. Janet says: 'It is vital that nothing is missed and every look and emotion is noticed: when the bride's father sees his daughter dressed in her gown for the first time, the cameraman should be there; when the groom turns to look at his bride as she enters the church, his reaction should be captured on film.'

How many camera operators?

Most companies will work with two camera operators: one to film the bride getting ready and leaving and the other to be at the ceremony with shots of the groom and guests arriving. Janet says: 'The first camera should manage to capture all the special moments of the morning: the bride putting on her earrings, fastening her shoes, her father popping the champagne cork. A second camera covers the groom's preparations and emotions, allowing the couple to have a record of the entire day and experience moments that they would have otherwise missed or forgotten about in the excitement of the day.' Some companies insist on using two camera operators; however others will work with one and the fee will reflect this.

Top tip

Wedding video experts Janet Fenton and Alan Howard both reiterate once again that you shouldn't be impressed solely by the equipment of the company. Alan says: 'David Bailey could do a good job using only an old-fashioned Brownie; it is the person behind the camera, not the camera itself which determines whether the finished product is simply mediocre or fantastic.' He also advises that a couple should insist on watching an entire wedding video – from start to finish – from the video company's portfolio. It is very easy to produce a compilation of the best shots for potential clients to view, which is not a true representation of their work.

the entertainment

In this chapter you will learn:

- **how to book a band/discotheque**
- **suggestions for entertainment**
- **how to deal with agencies**
- **ideas for hymns**
- **suggestions for Civil Ceremony music**
- **how to entertain the children.**

Once the venue and the photographer are booked, one of the most important and crucial elements of the wedding is the entertainment: 'If music be the food of love play on!'

Bands

An exciting jazz band playing swing numbers from Frank Sinatra, Dean Martin and Ella Fitzgerald when guests arrive at the reception will get everyone in the party mood, or a classical string quartet playing gently on the terrace of a stately home, while guests sip champagne on a gorgeous summer's day, creates a divinely serene atmosphere. However, it is notoriously difficult to find a suitable band for an event, unless you have been at a party where a particular artist has been working and you have been able to ascertain first-hand whether they would be right for your personal taste and requirements.

Finding a band

All the bridal magazines have advertisements in their classified sections for bands, discotheques and entertainers, some of which will have brochures and CDs to send to you: others may have the added bonus of a DVD to showcase their recent work. If you are happy with the style and cost quoted, it would still be a good idea to ask for some references so that you can verify their own promotional material and speak to past clients about their professionalism and repertoire.

Going to see a band play

If it is at all possible, before you go ahead and book them, ask to see the band in action. If they are a popular band/artist they should have some gigs in the near future in a central location that you could check out. Some bands have reservations about inviting potential clients to a private function, as they feel that it would somehow be intrusive; assure them that you will watch discreetly from a distance to see how they present themselves and perhaps arrange to meet with them in their break or at the end of the show to discuss your own particular needs. They are usually happy with this arrangement, particularly if they are playing at a corporate event, which is more appropriate for a viewing.

Discotheques

The advantage of employing the services of a DJ and discotheque is that you will be able to choose your favourite music and have the original artists singing the tracks. When you use a professional company, they will ask you for your preferred playlist and ensure that they have a good range of the music: if they are unable to supply a certain song, they should inform you prior to the day. The latest computerized sound and lighting systems are used by most of the proficient organizations, ensuring that the dancing area looks and sounds like a state-of-the-art nightclub!

Dance floors/lighting/sound

Smoke, lasers, haze, bubbles and UV lighting are all additional options to transform your discotheque into a venue fit for the Ibiza clubbing scene! LED dance floors (floors lit from underneath and programmed to whatever colour theme you require) are available to hire which will add an exciting dimension to the dancing and impress your guests as they party the night away. Alternative styles on the market, such as black and white chequerboard designs, give a huge variety of choice.

Top tip

Always make sure that you discuss the running order of your wedding with the actual DJ who will be attending the wedding, so that they are completely aware of your requirements. They should also be able to provide you with radio microphones to use during the speeches, which can be useful if a member of your bridal party does not feel confident enough to project their voice to a large gathering and needs some assistance.

Agencies

Entertainment agencies also advertise widely on the internet and through the trade magazines and are a good source of information. Although you will be paying an additional fee to cover their commission, you have some recourse should there be any problems on the day. There are agencies that showcase their clients' work on the internet, so you can watch their performances from the comfort of your home and listen to the quality of the artists. A word of warning: although the majority of these recordings are genuine, unfortunately there is also the potential for them to be misleading and therefore a visit to witness for yourself the authenticity of the group/individual is always advisable.

Adam Sternberg, Director of entertainment agency Sternberg Clarke advises that: 'When approaching an agency, a couple should keep an open mind on the style of entertainment they would like, as there are so many options available, it would be unfortunate not to listen to a professional's ideas and thoughts for your particular event.'

Icebreaker act

Adam often suggests to clients that they consider having an 'icebreaker act' at the reception, while the photographs are being taken. He explains: 'At this point, your guests have not yet had a drink and may not feel confident in a social situation where they do not know many others, and by bringing in a novelty act such as a strolling musician, a slight-of-hand magician, or even a look-a-like for a themed event, most people will react well and begin to relax and have fun!' Naturally the budget will determine whether these options are feasible: however, these artists are not particularly expensive and they will make a significant difference to the atmosphere of the party, making a memorable impact to the day.

Musical tastes

Another point to remember is that when choosing your music for the DJ or band, it is important to consider your guests' as well as your own personal taste. Adam says: 'If you are really into Goth Metal, it may not be the best idea to play this style of music all night, especially as you will probably have a range of generations at the wedding. By all means incorporate it into the evening, but also make sure that you play a varied repertoire, so all your guests are able to enjoy themselves!'

Playlist

Do not be too specific in your playlist. Do let your DJ know which song you would like as the first dance and perhaps the last dance; if you provide him/her with a full list of songs you would like played in strict order, you will restrict the creativity and control of the dance floor, as they need to gauge the mood of the group and decide on the order themselves.

Cultural music

Use entertainment to put your own personal mark on the wedding. For example, if you are not from the UK, why not incorporate music from your own country and culture? It would be fabulous to employ a Ceilidh band if you are from the Scottish Highlands, a rousing Welsh choir in the church, or a violin and accordion playing traditional Irish folk music.

Dance lessons

With the recent trend for dancing, Adam says that it is becoming very popular for couples to have a few classes before the wedding, to ensure that the first dance they perform in front of all their family and friends is done with confidence and flair! You do not have to be Fred Astaire and Ginger Rogers, but even by knowing a few moves and being familiar with your chosen song, a dance teacher can show you how to hold yourself and impress the gathered crowd. If confident, you may even choose to re-enact a scene from a film to entertain your thrilled guests!

Booking the artist

When you have met and decided on a band or artist, ensure that you discuss all your expectations of them. If you have booked the reception/ceremony at a venue such as a hotel, you should ensure that the management liaise with the entertainer to confirm arrangements direct. If you are hiring a private venue and managing them yourselves, there are a number of points you should confirm.

- **What time will they arrive and set up?** You should make sure that the band have set up their equipment at least one hour before you and your guests are due to arrive at the venue. You do not want them arriving late and having to bring in their equipment, passing your guests on the way!
- **Check their playlist to ensure that the music is your choice.** They will be able to give you a good indication of the tracks they plan to include; however, if there is a particular song that is a favourite or if there is one that you do not want played at all for any reason, make sure they are aware of this in good time.
- **Ask about their costumes.** If you have seen them live, you will probably know what style they will be wearing, but it is

always useful to ask – especially if the wedding is black tie and you would like them to complement the dress code.

- **Contact details.** If you have booked a DJ or band through an agent, always ask for their contact details so that you can give them a call and have an informal chat. This is a great way of introducing yourselves and getting to know the person who will be in charge of your entertainment. Also ensure you have their mobile number for the day itself: you never know when or why you may have to contact them, so make sure you have all the details to hand.
- **Finalize payment terms.** Are you expected to pay on the night, or is the balance due after the wedding?

Marvellous music!

There is a plethora of talented bands, musicians and singers across the length and breadth of the country offering superb and skilled entertainment for your wedding day.

Harpist

Most harpists are well trained and of a similar standard, so viewing is not always necessary.

Tribute band

These are very popular for larger weddings as they work especially well when you have a greater number of guests to entertain. They are great for themed weddings, providing familiar songs from a particular era (for example, Abba, Beatles, Elvis).

Classical trio/quartet

The majority of classically trained musicians are of a similar standard, and will provide a broad repertoire of music.

Jazz vocals and band

There is a trend for smooth dinner jazz to be played during the meal and vocalists tend to vary in quality and style, so it is advisable to view them in person before booking.

Function band

An excellent function band will be able to play a wide selection of all the well-known hits which will cater for guests of all ages. It is advisable to view bands in person before booking them.

Barn dance

Barn dances are a great way to get all your guests dancing together and perfect for a country setting with a reception held in the open air, or in a barn. Agencies can provide these bands and standards will vary.

Professional singer

You may choose to employ the services of a professional singer, either for the church service or civil ceremony during the signing of the register, or at the reception during or after dinner. Discuss your favourite songs with the artist before the booking and ask for a list of their repertoire and, if possible, a CD.

Guitar soloist

If you are planning a wedding with a Spanish or Latin theme – perhaps you are serving tapas instead of canapés – it would be fantastic to have a Spanish guitarist serenade your guests as they experience the atmosphere of Andalucia.

Steel band

A tropical beach wedding would not be complete without the sounds of a Caribbean steel band, to fill the air with the calypso beat. Equally a summer wedding in the UK, in the garden of a private house, would come alive with the exciting music a steel band produces.

Other suggestions

- Opera singer
- Gypsy jazz band
- Brazilian and Salsa band
- Mexican Mariachi band
- Gypsy King style bands
- Russian folk band
- Ceilidh band
- Cabaret performer

Church music

Your minister or priest will be able to introduce you to the resident organist, or put you in touch with local professionals who will be able to play the hymns you have chosen. If possible, always meet the organist before the day so that you can go through any thoughts or preferences you may have.

You will need to choose the pieces you would like played at certain points of the service – for example, the bride's entrance, signing of the register and the bride's exit. The 'Wedding March' from Lohengrin ('Here Comes the Bride') used to be the main piece played for the entrance of the bride; there are many more choices available which would be suitable for either the entrance or the exit.

Choirs

Check the availability of a resident choir with your minister at the earliest opportunity, as sometimes a professional group may sing at other venues and it would be a great pity if a good choir was based at the church where you were getting married and they were booked elsewhere on your date. If the church does not have its own choir, it is possible to arrange your own; bear in mind the additional cost which could escalate depending on the size of the group.

Choosing your church music

Catherine Francoise of Wedding Songs says: 'Music can enhance the mood and feeling of the most memorable events of your life. Whether you decide to have a professional singer, a stylish pianist, beautiful harpist or a majestic organist, the songs and music played at your wedding will live in your own memory and that of your guests forever.'

Hymns or songs?

There are usually two or three hymns or songs sung during a wedding service. If you are able to choose hymns that are familiar to your family and friends, you will have a church filled with music and joyful sounds, instead of embarrassed glances between the congregation and very little noise! Here is a selection of popular wedding tunes, both religious and non-religious.

Traditional hymns

'All Things Bright and Beautiful'
'O, Praise Ye the Lord'
'Lord of All Hopefulness'
'Jerusalem'
'Dear Lord and Father of Mankind'
'Praise my Soul the King of Heaven'
'Come Down O Love Divine'
'Father Hear the Prayer we Offer'
'Give me Joy in my Heart'
'Love Divine all Loves Excelling'
'Make me a Channel of your Peace'
'One More Step Along the World I Go'

Classical non-religious wedding songs

'Solo Con Te' (Handel)
'Caro Mio Ben' (Handel)
'Eternal Source Of Light Divine' (Handel)
'Ombra Mai Fu' (Handel)
'Bailero' (Canteloube)
'In Trutina – Carmina Burana' (Orff)

Operatic songs

'O Mio Babbino Caro' (Puccini)
'Lakme Flower Song' (Delibes)
'Lascia ch'io Pianga' (Handel)
'Soave Sia II Vento' (Mozart)
'Depuis Le Jour' (Charpentier)
'L'Amero' (Mozart)

Jazz songs

'Fly Me To The Moon'
'I Only Have Eyes For You'
'Our Love Is Here To Stay'
'Our Love Affair'
'Love Walked In'
'I Get A Kick Out Of You'
'Someone To Watch Over Me'
'Meet The Beat Of My Heart'
'Love Is The Sweetest Thing'

Musical theatre songs

'Come What May'
'All I Ask Of You'
'One Hand, One Heart'
'Can You Feel The Love Tonight?'
'Love Changes Everything'
'Somewhere'
'True Love'

Contemporary songs

'From This Moment'
'How Do I Live?'
'Heaven'
'I Dreamed Of You'
'Just One Lifetime'
'My Heart Will Go On'
'Kissing You (Love Theme Romeo and Juliet)'
'Because You Loved Me'
'Up Where We Belong'
'Have I Told You Lately That I Love You?'
'Bridge Over Troubled Water'
'Nothing's Gonna Change My Love For You'
'When You Tell Me That You Love Me'
'The First Time Ever I Saw Your Face'
'Battle Hymn Of Love'
'Truly, Madly, Deeply'
'Your Song'
'Woman In Love'
'And I Love You So'
'I Won't Last A Day'
'Always There'
'Without You'
'Get Here'
'Only Love'
'Close To You'
'We've Only Just Begun'
'Evergreen'
'Save The Best For Last'
'Love Me Tender'
'You Light Up My Life'
'Songbird'
'Because'

'I Believe'
'The Power Of Love'
'And I Love You So'
'Endless Love'
'The Wedding Song (Ave Maria)'
'Falling Into You'
'Irish Blessing'

Contemporary religious songs

'Our Shalom'
'Then Came A Friend'
'Love Has Never Been This Way Before'
'A Song For A Life Together'
'Two Flames That Glow'
'Wedding Song (There Is Love)'
'I Dreamed Of You'
'Flesh Of My Flesh'
'Wedding Prayer'
'He's Got The Whole World In His Hands'
'Where You Lead I Will Follow'
'Psalm 27'
'El Shadai'

Music for the ceremony

Before the ceremony

As your guests are arriving at the church, it is often a quiet, somewhat awkward time as people greet each other and the best man and groom stand nervously waiting for the bride to arrive. If you can therefore arrange some calm, peaceful background music to set the scene in a welcoming way and create a special mood for those arriving early, it is always very much appreciated. Usually the organist will oblige by playing from his repertoire of suitable pieces.

The bridesmaids' entrance

You may choose to have a soloist perform a lyrical piece as your bridesmaids enter the church and begin to process down the aisle.

The bride's entrance

These pieces are traditionally played by an organist – possibly with a trumpet player for a more dramatic sound – as the bride enters the church and walks down the aisle with her father. However, you may opt for a softer, more romantic piece such as 'Ave Maria' sung by a soloist to create a lyrical, mood. Some popular pieces are:

- 'The Prince of Denmark's March' (Clark)
- 'Wedding March' from *The Marriage of Figaro* (Mozart)
- 'Wedding March' ('Here comes the Bride') from *Lohengrin* (Wagner)
- 'Canon in D' (Pachelbel)
- 'Trumpet Tune in D' (Purcell)
- 'Salut d'amour' (Elgar)
- 'Hornpipe in D' from the *Water Music* (Handel)

Before or after the vows

Catherine Francoise suggests: 'You may choose a solo to enhance your vows or emphasize a reading or prayers, such as 'One Hand, One Heart', 'The Rose', or 'Pie Jesu' among others. This is also a special time for yourselves to listen to something sung 'just for you', which can be very moving.'

During communion

While communion is being taken, the pieces played could be 'Pie Jesu', 'Ave Maria', 'Laudate Dominium', 'Ave Verum', 'Amazing Grace', 'Make Me A Channel Of Your Peace' and 'Jesu Joy Of Man's Desiring', among others.

During the signing of the register

This formality can take a little time and if you have to leave the congregation to go to an adjoining room, guests are sometimes left in the church with little to do except wait and chat quietly. Rather than 'filling time', you could use this part of the wedding service to introduce another solo classical religious aria such as: Mozart's 'Alleluia', 'Exultate Jubilate' or Handel's 'Let the Bright Seraphim'. Romantic arias such as: Puccini's 'O Mio Babbino Caro' or the 'Lakme Flower Song' are other options. For a completely different modern romantic mood, you could choose appropriate songs by Celine Dion, Barbara Streisand or Shania Twain, etc.

As the couple exit

The organist and or any other musicians usually play the exit, as it is an excuse for a powerfully rousing piece to celebrate the occasion, such as:

- 1st movement from 'Brandenburg Concerto No. 3 in 'G' (Bach)
- 'Wedding March' from *A Midsummer Night's Dream* (Mendelssohn)
- 'Trumpet Voluntary – Op 6 No. 5' (Stanley)
- 'Libiamo no lieti calici' from *La Traviata* (Verdi)
- 'Radetsky March' (Strauss)
- 1st movement from 'Spring' from *The Four Seasons* (Vivaldi)

Catholic wedding music

There may be a choice to have a psalm sung in place of a reading such as Mozart's 'Laudate Dominium' (Psalm 116), 'The Lord's My Shepherd' or a beautiful contemporary psalm, for example Adrian Snell's 'Psalm 27', or the 'Lord's Prayer' (Our Father).

Civil ceremony music

The music you choose to have played at your civil ceremony must not contain any religious connotations and therefore it is important that you take advice from experts in this field. There are many companies advertising both on the internet and through wedding magazines who are able to provide the guidance and support you will need if you are concerned about choosing appropriate pieces for such a celebration. For more information about which pieces are allowed, contact:

Marriages & Civil Partnerships Section
General Register Office
Trafalgar Road
Southport
PR8 2HH
Tel: 0151 471 4814

Without music, a civil ceremony can be quite short; by adding music and poetry or prose, it will make the whole experience a more memorable, personal event.

A string quartet

An ideal choice for a civil ceremony can be a string quartet that could play as guests are arriving at the venue, when the bride enters, during the signing of the register and for the exit. They could also then move to another location to play during the drinks reception and wedding breakfast as their instruments and stands do not take up a great deal of space; being one of the most mobile and versatile of musicians, they are often one of the most popular choices. They are also able to play a huge range of styles, including both romantic and the jazzier, fun pieces.

A pianist

A pianist is also a good option, especially if the venue has its own piano. However he/she will generally be restricted to only play in the room where the piano is situated, unless it is possible to move it; therefore it may be difficult to hear the pianist if they are inside and the reception is taking place outside.

Gospel music

Recently there has been a new trend for gospel music at marriage services. Performing well-known numbers such as 'All You Need is Love' as your guests arrive at the venue and the ultimate romantic song, 'Endless Love', as you walk down the aisle, the gospel choir will treat your guests to a feast of indulgent sounds! Can you imagine hearing 'Signed, Sealed and Delivered' while you sign the register, then walk back up the aisle as a married couple to the incredibly infectious and rousing 'Oh Happy Day'? You may choose to continue the music theme by having the band sing in the background while the photographs are being taken following the ceremony and afterwards to keep the party mood at the drinks reception. Although gospel choirs are known to sing religious songs, which is not appropriate for a civil ceremony, they are also able to sing love songs and other upbeat numbers which are suitable for a civil marriage or partnership, and therefore they are an option to consider if you would like to have a boost of energy and soul at your wedding.

Alternative/additional entertainment

Sometimes wedding ceremonies take place quite early in the day and the meal could be taking place later in the afternoon, with an unavoidable extended time period in between. If this is the case, there are ways of filling in any awkward gaps when guests might feel at a loss! Perhaps you could arrange for a mini concerto to be performed, with guests invited to watch and enjoy the performance in the open air – weather permitting – or in an appropriate area of the venue? Strolling magicians performing slight-of-hand tricks are very popular with guests, as they baffle and amaze their audience. Caricaturists can create quick impressions of your guests and amuse their subjects as they recreate amusing caricatures of your friends and family.

Entertaining children at a wedding

If you plan to invite children to your wedding, it would be a sensible idea to have some entertainment arranged to keep them amused when you return from the church or in the gap between the ceremony and the wedding breakfast. Perhaps you could also have an appropriate entertainer available during the later part of the meal, when speeches have a tendency to drag on, and little ones become fidgety and bored. A bouncy castle erected in the grounds or in a suitable indoor space would keep them occupied and use some of that pent-up energy suppressed during the wedding ceremony! Clowns and puppet shows for the younger guests are always a good option, and will keep them together while the show goes on, so their parents can enjoy the remainder of their meal in peace.

For peace of mind always ensure that you choose a qualified and experienced company to look after the children. Kathryn Parry Brown, Director of Arty Animals, says: 'It is vital that the safety of the children is ensured and therefore a company that has been checked and passed by Ofsted (The Office for Standards in Education) will give you the reassurance you need.' She adds: 'Providing inspiring projects and craft activities to keep them occupied during the day, will stimulate their artistic abilities to create wonderful keepsakes themed around the wedding, such as icing and decorating mini wedding cakes, hearts and horseshoes, all while their parents are content in the knowledge that they are safe and well looked after.'

As an alternative, children could be provided with activity bags at the wedding to keep them busy, which may be colour-coordinated to match your scheme. Each one could contain a range of toys and activities such as wooden jigsaws, bracelet-making kits, stickers and colouring sets, all of which are not edible or messy in any way. Choose activities that won't make any noise; this is a blessing when you are limited with space and do not want too much disruption from the room with the little ones in it.

Firework displays

Can you imagine anything more spectacular than concluding the most perfect day of your lives with the wonder and excitement of a firework display? Imagine guests gathering in anticipation as they wait in the grounds of a magnificent stately home, which is a perfect backdrop for a skyline lit up with an array of colour, beauty and animation! Initially, check with the venue that it is permissible to arrange a firework display. When sourcing a suitable company to provide the pyrotechnics for your wedding, it is vital to ensure that they have the experience and qualifications necessary to supply a service which is both professional and safe; the potential consequences of any errors would be unthinkable.

Finding and employing a professional

It is vital that an experienced specialist company should be employed. Phoenix Fireworks suggests that when contacting a pyrotechnic company there are three main areas that you should check out, to verify their professionalism:

- Check on their insurance. They should have third party firework insurance which should be confirmed when you book them and independently verified by checking the following website: www.fireworkindustryregister.co.uk.
- They should be affiliated to the BPA – British Pyrotechnics Association. This qualification proves that their staff have passed all the relevant tests. You can also check an individual firer's qualifications by logging on to www.bpa-fmg.org.uk.
- Ask how many years experience they have. If they have been trading for less than five years it is advisable to choose one with more years of proven experience.

If the budget permits, the world of pyrotechnics can be spectacularly extravagant. Displays with the wow factor, synchronized to music chosen by yourselves could leave you with a hefty bill, particularly if you have your heart set on a display staged around water, such as fountains and lakes. Nevertheless, the lasting memory it provides may be worth the outlay! Perhaps you are having your reception aboard a boat? Imagine the scene: as the boat glides down the waterway, it slows to the sight of a fabulous surprise firework display from the banks of the river, amazing and entertaining all your guests!

Fireworks to music

As the ultimate in drama and showmanship, why not have a display set to a live 40–50 piece orchestra lasting up to 25 minutes? A complete sound and lighting system for the band, performing together with the fireworks as a pyro-musical will undoubtedly leave you with an experience you will never forget.

Colours and gimmicks

The colours of the fireworks could be co-ordinated with your theme: for example, a gold or silver display, multicoloured or pastels. The shows can accommodate all age ranges and can even omit noisy fireworks if these are offensive to any of your younger or older guests. As a finale, your names can be lit up in fireworks, or 'Mr and Mrs' displayed with hearts, champagne bottles and many other themed options. Why not speed off to your honeymoon driving through an avenue of explosive fireworks to the delight of family and friends?

12 wedding transport

In this chapter you will learn:

- the available options for wedding transport
- a checklist of questions to ask your supplier
- unusual modes of transport.

A Rolls Royce or a rickshaw? One of the leading factors in your choice of wedding transport will be the distance you need to travel between the church or wedding ceremony and the reception venue. You may have dreamed of trotting down a country lane in an elegant horse-drawn carriage, or perhaps you would absolutely love for you and your new husband to drive to the reception in an open-top sports car with your veil flowing behind you in the summer breeze! Whatever your choice of transport, there are many points to consider.

Cars

Vintage cars

A wonderful vintage Rolls Royce or Bentley is still a popular choice for weddings. The condition of these vehicles is paramount as the potential for disappointment is high, due to the cost involved in keeping them in tip-top shape! Unfortunately, there are companies who own vehicles which have lapsed into disrepair and they continue to offer these cars for weddings, despite the shoddy upholstery, peeling paintwork and unprofessionally-attired drivers! Numerous vintage car suppliers have websites and brochures which look very glossy and impressive, showing high-quality interiors of their cars, shiny paintwork and glowing recommendations from past customers. Many of these are genuine and do offer fantastic services; however it is extremely important that you visit the car supplier in person and view the actual car you have chosen. You will then be able to have a good look at the vehicle and actually sit inside to judge whether there will be enough room for a billowing wedding dress; some of the older vintage models have limited interior space, so it is vital to ensure that there is sufficient leg and dress room! Often these vintage vehicles are privately owned and leased to companies who supply the chauffeurs for the day. In this case, you might have to arrange to see the car at the house or garage of the owner.

Top tip

Always ensure that the company supplying the driver has confirmed in writing exactly which car you have booked, with the make, model and registration. Occasionally the cars are not available to view in the garage, or perhaps are kept too far away from your home to warrant the travelling involved to see them. In this case, you can always ask if you can arrange to meet the driver at a wedding or event in a central location where you will then be able to see it 'at work' and check on its condition while it is being used.

Other popular wedding cars

There are a huge range of wedding cars available for hire, and each bride and groom will have their personal favourite, including: vintage Jaguars (coupé, saloon and convertible), limousines, Ford Open Tourers, Rolls Royces (Lagonda, Phantom III, Landaulette) and pre-war Austins. A modern classic is The Love Bug, a new version of the old 'Herbie' car: a new cream Beetle Cabriolet with leather interior, decorated with ribbons to match your colour scheme.

Cars featured in TV and film

Cars featured in well-known television programmes or films are increasingly being used for weddings, as the prestige of telling everyone that you rode in a famous car to your wedding is very appealing. There are specialist suppliers of vehicles to the film and television industry, and many of these offer their cars to the public. It will probably involve a few telephone calls and negotiation skills to secure the car of your dreams – perhaps Chitty Chitty Bang Bang is your all-time favourite!

Limousines

We all secretly yearn to be film stars it seems, and one way of experiencing the glamour and excitement of the movies is to hire a stretch limousine for your wedding, complete with laser lighting, fully-equipped bar, television, DVD and music! White is the most sought-after colour for weddings, with shocking pink and executive black limousines becoming more in demand to transport guests – accommodating up to 18 at a time. The American stretched Hummer limousine and Jeep 4x4 are funkier, more substantial vehicles and look perfect in the photos for an evening party at a sassy nightclub. Once again, it is imperative to check the vehicle's condition. One bride-to-be visited a reputable firm only to find the carpeting threadbare, spotlights hanging loosely from the ceiling and the television broken! Thankfully she had allowed sufficient time to be able to source another company, but this may not always be the case, which is why it is vital to visit your supplier early on in the preparations.

Checklist of questions to ask your car supplier

- Will the driver be uniformed?
- Do they supply flowers and if so, are they fresh or silk? Can you ask for a particular colour scheme? Is there an extra cost involved?
- Do they have a back-up vehicle in case of breakdown? What replacement car will be supplied?
- Will they be checking any road closures on the day due to marches/demonstrations or other road works, which may cause delay to the journey?
- Will ribbons be supplied? Can you choose the colour?
- Do they supply champagne for the bride and groom?
- Ask to see their portfolio of weddings – they should have photographs taken of their previous jobs which will show how professional and well turned out the chauffeur is.
- Check and always allow sufficient time to book your car. Bear in mind that some of the more popular vintage models will be snapped up months before the wedding date – especially if they are in a popular colour, such as cream or white.

Horse and carriage

How civilized to trot along in a Landau, an open-top horse and carriage, on a glorious summers day, sipping champagne and waving to onlookers. Many couples still choose to book this mode of transport, as it evokes images of the innocence of a bygone era, of Jane Austen's *Pride and Prejudice*, when romance and gallantry was the order of the day and women were wooed and seduced by handsome fellows in frock coats and leather boots. Before you get carried away by the romance of it all, here are some points to consider!

- If all is perfect and you are fortunate with the weather, this can be an ideal way to travel. However, it is wise to be realistic and make sure that the carriage you have reserved has the ability to convert into one with a covered roof, for inclement weather.

- The majority of suppliers should have experienced staff to ride on the coach with an additional driver or groomsman suitably attired and completely in control of the horses in any situation, either on town or country roads.
- Suppliers should survey any new routes and check the terrain for steep hills and so on, as well as ensuring that they are aware of suitable horsebox parking areas.
- It is recommended that a journey should be no longer than 2–3 miles, as a 2-mile journey can take approximately 20 minutes by carriage. The supplier will bring the horse to the starting location by horsebox and set up the carriage near to the venue, so that it saves any additional lengthy journeys for the horse.
- Alternatively, if the journey from the church or ceremony to the reception venue is too long for the horse's comfort, it can be arranged for a car to take you part of the journey and at a designated place, you swap over and arrive in style in a leisurely carriage ride.

Prevent a disaster – always make a personal visit!

Having provisionally booked a horse and carriage, a couple arranged with the supplier to view it at a wedding, prior to confirming the booking. On arriving they found that the driver of the carriage was sitting on a wall outside the church, drinking from a bottle of beer and the horse was wondering around the courtyard on its own, pulling a carriage that was in such a bad state of repair that the leather roof was torn and slit and the upholstery was dirty and shabby! Needless to say that particular booking did not go ahead!

Unusual transport

White stallion

Some Asian weddings will enjoy the spectacle of the groom arriving on a white stallion horse, bejewelled with rich embroidery and leading a procession of family and friends to the sound of a Bollywood drummer!

Scooby Doo van

'Scooby Dooby Doo, We love you!' Remember the 'Mystery Machine' featured in the films and cartoons? This is available for the young-at-heart to hire, seating eight inside for a fun mode of transport for a themed event.

Fire engine

How about a converted fire engine limousine, seating up to 14 in a customized interior, complete with fireplace (what better place to have one!), smoke machine, strobe lighting and a 32" television screen, to show all your favourite pop and music videos on the way to the party!

Hot air balloon

Nothing could be more spectacularly elegant than to arrive at the venue like a bird, gliding gently down from the clouds, landing in the grounds of a stately home, surrounded by thrilled friends and family! Ensure that you are booking through a reputable firm. Bailey Balloons advise that: 'A popular choice is to supply a tethered balloon in the grounds of the venue. Guests in small groups of two or three can climb into the basket to be elevated up into the air for a short ride; it's often the chance of a lifetime to fly high above the ground in a hot air balloon. Alternatively, the couple can be whisked away into the air after the reception, waved off by all their guests for an hour's flight. They will then be brought down close to the hotel or their next destination.'

London double-decker bus

Traditional red London open- and closed-top Routemaster buses have been seen around the capital for many years, carrying wedding guests to the venue in a fun and relaxed style. The names of the couple along with a good luck message can be displayed at the front of the bus and the interior is usually decorated with balloons and ribbons to add to the party spirit – although check with your supplier when making the booking whether they will be doing this, or if they expect you to arrange for the labour and materials.

These buses are always a good choice as they are able to carry up to 65–72 passengers at a time, therefore accommodating a large number of guests travelling together eliminating the anxiety of finding their own way to the venue and the potential parking restrictions they may encounter.

There are companies who privately own and customize buses, combining the history and familiarity of the vehicle with the luxury of comfortable seating in leather upholstery; some of the older, less well-maintained versions may snag or damage wedding attire. It is a fabulous way to get to know each other and to be able to socialize on the way to the wedding while chatting and listening to music via a state-of-the-art sound system and being served champagne by the on-board hostess! Sometimes even the couple themselves opt to travel aboard with their family and friends, not wanting to miss out on any of the fun!

London taxis

London taxis are synonymous with the city and therefore if the wedding is taking place centrally, what is more appropriate than to travel in a traditional London cab? There are companies which have a network of contacts to provide a number of black or white London taxis at the same time. This will need to be co-ordinated and confirmed well in advance of the date, so that the individual drivers are available and there will generally be an additional charge to keep the taxis free. However, overall this can sometimes work out as a less expensive option, and a good photo opportunity with identical taxis all lined up (with ribbons) waiting to ferry your guests to the reception (five people maximum per cab). Vintage London taxis, such as the pre- and post-war styles and the Asquith replica vintage models, are always in demand and often need booking well in advance. They combine the look and feel of a bygone age with the modern day engine, ensuring a trouble-free journey.

Transport on a budget

If funds are needed elsewhere it is possible to cut the costs of transport by using friends and family to provide vehicles. Perhaps you have a relative who has an enthusiasm for cars and can supply his own unique 'pride and joy' for the day? The taxi is a modern and inexpensive way of travelling (especially in London, as previously mentioned). If you discuss your requirements with a city firm, you should be able to book a number of taxis in advance and they should all turn up at the same time to take your guests to their destination. If taxis are required at the end of the evening to take guests back to their hotel or home, it is advisable to book these early in the day, as Friday and Saturday night is their busiest time and you do not want your guests left waiting, or at worst stranded, without means of getting home.

Top tip

Make sure that the best man has the contact numbers for the drivers of the vehicles on the day of the wedding. One worrying incident occurred when the wedding cars dropped the bridal party off at the church and unfortunately left the bridesmaids' flowers in the back of the car; this could have turned into a disaster, were it not for the best man's quick thinking! The girls returned to where they had been left just 10 minutes before, but realized that the cars had been driven off with their flowers without any means of contacting the drivers! Needless to say there was a degree of panic on everyone's behalf. The best man suggested that maybe the drivers had gone for a break and he ran around the local cafés trying to find them – fortunately he stumbled on them having a cup of tea and reading the paper! Thankfully the bouquets were speedily retrieved and returned to the bridesmaids just in time to walk down the aisle. The advice therefore is to always ensure that you are able to contact all suppliers on their mobile phones in case of any unforeseen circumstances.

13 first night stays

In this chapter you will learn:

- **ideas for first night stays**
- **ideas for honeymoon destinations**
- **a six-month honeymoon countdown**
- **tips for packing your suitcase.**

Where to stay on your wedding night

Traditionally newly-weds would leave the reception quite early on in the evening for their honeymoon destination that same night. The trend over the past few years has been that – as so much time, effort and sheer love has been invested by the couple in the preparation for the wedding day – they are often reluctant to leave the festivities and are more likely to stay partying until the bitter end, making their exit only a short while before their guests! In this case it is usual to book into a nearby hotel for the first night and leave for the honeymoon destination fresh in the morning. Alternatively, they may choose to stay even longer, perhaps for the whole weekend and enjoy the company of family and friends who may have travelled long distances to be with them. This way, they are able to share more time with them once the hectic schedule of the day is over, and so perhaps travel later in the week.

Castle

For the ultimate in romance, a gothic-style castle set in magnificent grounds, with sumptuous, elegant bedrooms and delicious cuisine, is perfect for the first night of your married life together. Many historic castles have been converted into successful establishments offering luxurious accommodation in exceptionally beautiful locations, perfect for winding down after the hectic schedule of the wedding day. Finding one such hotel near an airport has its advantages as you will be able to relax and recuperate, then be driven the short distance to catch your plane to your honeymoon destination.

Honeymooners can usually expect to be pampered with bath robes, slippers and luxury toiletries on their first night as husband and wife, so make sure you take full advantage.

Chic city hotel

Following a chic city wedding why not choose to opt for the timeless elegance of a quiet urban hotel, with fabulous views from your penthouse executive suite providing an oasis of calm after the excitement of the day?

Country decadence

The Lake District in Cumbria gives you the opportunity of wonderfully picturesque surroundings and quaint stonewalled exclusive hotels, for pure privacy and romance.

Luxury hotel groups

Choosing a hotel from a renowned group of luxury residences should guarantee prestigious accommodation, gourmet dining and a high standard of quality and service. Spending your first night in one such property will certainly swathe you in memories to savour and cherish.

Scottish serenity

Scotland is home to many award-winning hotels – some at the foothills of the Highlands – and would be a wonderful place to spend a romantic night or weekend before jetting off to a warmer climate.

Fabulous honeymoon destinations

See the Taking it further section for full details and websites.

Los Angeles, USA

With its relaxed Californian attitude, Beverly Hills is one of Hollywood's hottest destinations for a honeymoon. Relax in a poolside cabana, complete with flatscreen TV and personal ipod, or lounge on one of their hotel's Moroccan-style pool beds and enjoy some shade before heading for the shops on Rodeo Drive, only minutes away from your suite. A private dinner in your room or hiking in the Santa Monica Mountains with a picnic provided by the hotel, or a sunset cruise in Marina del Rey will ensure a LA honeymoon to remember.

Oman and Dubai

Resorts in Oman and Dubai are renowned for their luxury and decadence. Once you have both been refreshed and revitalized from your journey, you may be ready to experience the exotic, exciting markets or ultra-modern shopping malls, soak up the Arabian sunshine with a trip into the dessert or simply absorb the ambience of your hotel, with its sprawling palm gardens and beachside setting.

Channel Islands

The captivating mix of British and French cultures attracts honeymooners to all five Channel Islands: Jersey, Guernsey, Sark, Alderney and Herm. The warm, mild climate ensures that newly-weds can participate in a wide range of outdoor activities, from hiking to golf, to windsurfing and sunbathing! This tax-free zone charms the rich and famous, which in turn promotes sassy restaurants, chic hotels and duty-free shopping. Horse-drawn carriages are seen on the roads banned from cars, and spectacular beaches and panoramic views offer a feast of pleasure. Fourteenth-century manor houses converted into fine hotels will lavish champagne and homemade shortbread on their very special guests.

France

The heart of rural Provence is a fabulous place to visit and explore on your honeymoon, with a surprising mix of traditional French architecture and intimate chic boutique hotels with their retro style of furnishings and strong, vibrant colours in their suites. Contemporary artwork appeals to the discerning client and attracts foodies, as the cuisine is exquisite! With 50 varieties of sun-gorged tomatoes and wine from the Rhine, Luberon and Provence you are assured a gastronomic experience to cherish! Activities in the local area include: bike riding, rock climbing, archery, bird of prey flying and the Avignon Theatre Festival.

Italy

The epitome of tranquillity, hotels renowned for their excellence and impeccable service are located on one of the most beautiful lakes in Italy. Lago Mergozzo, in the northern region, has a spectacular view of the sleepy village of Mergozzo set on a backdrop of mountains reflected in the still, fresh water. The private gardens of the hotels are an oasis of peaceful elegance, where you can lie watching the handful of windsurfers gently pass by enjoying the summer breezes while you indulge in a creamy cappuccino or two! Stresa and the nearby towns are steeped in architectural elegance and beauty, and visiting the islands Isola Bella, Isola Pescatori and Isola Madre is an experience not to be missed! Only one hour from the Alps, you will also be able to take a cable car ride up into the heights of the Macunaga Mountains, where the beauty and splendour of the pine trees and glaciers will provide wonderful memories of your time in this fascinating region of Italy.

Cornwall

Luxury cottages set in landscape designed gardens, and sports activities are found in abundance in craggy Cornwall. It is a perfect location for a honeymoon, with its rugged coastline, where you can be surfing in the morning and sailing on the south coast later in the same day!

Ireland

Forget the decadence of a honeymoon in a luxurious hotel where your every whim is pandered to! Why not get out in the fresh air and walk off some of those wedding cake calories by arranging a completely different holiday – striding out over the beautiful and dramatic Irish terrain! Savour the delights of the Emerald Isle, as you familiarize yourselves with the local ecology, history, culture, customs and folklore, while rambling through some of the most spectacular terrain you will ever encounter.

Honeymoon countdown

Six months before

- Set a budget.
- Start discussing where your ideal fantasy honeymoon would be. This will allow for any research that will need to be done via the internet, travel operators, friends and family and travel publications.
- Find a travel agent who specializes in your destination, for example an adventure holiday, scuba diving trip or cruise, and discuss costs, options and any medical requirements of the country involved; vaccinations may be necessary months in advance of the trip.
- Research hotels, check room availability, reserve any rental cars.
- Book your tickets and any special seating arrangements – check luggage allowances.

Three months before

- Arrange any passports or visas if necessary. You do not have to change your name when you get married.
- If you do change your name on marriage, you will need to amend your passport to your married name before travelling abroad. Some countries may not accept an un-amended passport, even if you carry your marriage certificate with you. You should check the legal requirements at your travel office or the country's consulate in question. The change in name on the passport can be arranged up to three months before the wedding, although you will not be able to travel using the passport until the actual day of your marriage, so ensure that you check your diary for any pre-planned trips before the big day!
- The new passport will be valid for ten years and up to a further nine months depending on the remaining validity.
- Check travel insurance via the travel operator, independent companies, or your credit card company. If you travel more than twice a year, it is worth taking an annual policy. E111 for medical cover in Europe has been replaced by the European Health Insurance Card (EHIC), for more information contact www.dh.gov.uk

Two months before

- Check if you need to buy any new luggage – you may have included luggage on your gift list; check with the supplier whether it has been purchased and if so, arrange early delivery so you can use it for your honeymoon.
- Confirm with your gift list company that they will not be making any deliveries while you are away.
- Buy travel essentials such as toiletry bag, voltage converter and a travel iron.
- Make sure your camera is in good working order and you have sufficient sets of films and batteries if necessary. Buy or borrow a video camera and check that you know how it works.
- Research any tours, theatre tickets or any other activities that need prior booking – your travel agent should be able to provide this information.
- If you have any pets, for example cats or dogs, make arrangements for kennelling or confirm that neighbours will be in charge of their welfare.

One month before

- Write up a list of everything you need to pack, including clothes, toiletries and accessories. Buy items such as sunscreen, so there is no last-minute panic when you arrive at your destination.
- Reconfirm all reservations.
- Make a copy of your travel itinerary, including any phone, fax or email details; leave it with friends or family in case of an emergency.
- Ensure you have sufficient supplies of any medication you might need on the trip, for example migraine tablets, allergy pills, asthma inhalers, glasses, contact lenses. Carry all medication in their original prescription bottles to avoid questions at Customs.

Two weeks before

- Collect travel tickets and all applicable vouchers from your travel agent. Read all relevant material to double-check details are correct.
- Buy travellers cheques; make a note of the numbers in a separate place in the event that they are stolen.
- Exchange a small amount of money, for example £50, in the currency of the country you will be visiting, to cover any taxi fares or other expenses on arrival.

One week before

- Arrange to have your mail collected by a neighbour or held at the Post Office so that you do not have any left on the doorstep or in the letter box. The same applies to any other deliveries, for example milk, newspaper; cancel these for the duration of your trip.
- Set out clothes to pack – buy last-minute items.
- Get in touch with your house- or cat-sitter to reconfirm details, hand over the keys and give them a copy of your vet's number and your contact information.
- Buy any magazines or books for the trip.
- Make sure you have your address book for sending postcards to family and friends.
- Double-check that your luggage has your name and home address and the destination address details clearly attached.
- Check your mobile phone can roam globally or buy a foreign SIM card and cut out roaming charges.

Two days before departure

- Pack your suitcase.
- Use space-saving tips – for example, buy travel-size shampoo, conditioner, and toiletries.
- Pack your tickets, passport and money in your hand luggage.
- For plane travel, check-in online up to 24 hours ahead to avoid airport queues.
- Arrange for your luggage to be collected to save check-in queues at the airport.

Day of departure

- If travelling by air, be sure to arrive at the airport early to allow for security checks – a minimum of one hour before domestic flights, two hours for international.
- Drink plenty of water on the plane so that you arrive fresh and hydrated.
- Get on the local time as soon as you arrive at the airport, even if that means drinking coffee to stay awake. The sooner you adjust the better.

Relax and have fun! You're married, the wedding is over, and all you have to do now is enjoy each other and your well-deserved honeymoon!

Top tip

Always make sure you have informed your hotel that you are honeymooners as they will invariably give you special treatment with a few additional luxuries in the room or at dinner, if you are lucky. Why not make the most of it – you are only on honeymoon once in your life – we hope!

Packing your suitcase

Packing a suitcase is a strategic exercise in maximizing space and minimizing wrinkles.

Order of packing larger items

- Shirts at the bottom, then dresses, then trousers.
- Stack tops unfolded: place wrinkle-prone tops toward the bottom of a pile and the less delicate ones towards the top.
- Fold the sleeves in toward the shirts' torsos.
- Fold the shirts in half from the bottom. You now have a rectangular bundle of shirts – place in suitcase.
- Drape long dresses in the suitcase so that the ends hang over the sides.
- Place trousers and skirts on a flat surface and fold each in half lengthwise.
- Stack trousers and skirts on top of one another, with the easily wrinkled ones on the bottom and the more robust, such as jeans, on top. Fold the stack over so that its length is halved.
- Place your stack of trousers and skirts on top of the dresses, next fold the ends of the dresses over the trousers and skirts.

Packing accessories

- Roll ties loosely.
- Stuff socks in shoes, pack underwear in mesh laundry bags or side pockets to save space.
- Arrange each pair of shoes so that the heel of one aligns with the toe of the other.
- Wrap pairs of shoes in separate plastic bags and place them along the border of your suitcase.
- Protect clothes from leaks by placing toiletries in a plastic bag.
- Pack essential toiletries in hand luggage. Include your toothbrush, toothpaste, make-up, medication and other important items. Always check with your airline before packing to confirm which items are allowed in hand luggage.

Top tip

Avoid packing money, jewellery, travel documents, medication, keys and other valuables in your suitcase. Carry these items with you at all times.

14 happily ever after

In this chapter you will learn:

- **jobs to do on returning home – gifts/photos/video**
- **how to change your name**
- **how to make a will**
- **whether to store or sell the wedding dress**
- **the art of compromise**
- **tips for keeping the passion alive**
- **how to renew your vows.**

Returning home

With the excitement and romance of the honeymoon over, there is still plenty to look forward to in the coming days and weeks following one of the happiest and busiest periods of your life! Now is the time to reflect on the wedding day and the joy and emotions of a very special occasion with many aspects of the day still to enjoy and cherish.

Wedding gifts

Any gifts brought to your wedding will probably have been collected by the best man or your family and kept ready for your return. The bulk of the delivery from a gift list company should be arranged for a date when you will be able to receive them: contact them and confirm when your goods will arrive. If any gifts have been broken in transit, claim on your wedding insurance as soon as possible. Make sure that you write and send your thank you notes.

Your photographs

If you have not done so already, book a date to meet with your photographer to view the prints and to choose your favourites. This is a thrilling time, as you will have your own memories of the events of the day; however, when faced with an array of fresh new images, it will reignite a plethora of emotions. If the photographer has done their job well, they should have captured many scenes of which you were unaware, providing exciting surprises and creating your own personal story of the day.

The video/film

Hopefully the company you employed to film your wedding will have sent a copy of the DVD or video for your approval. Set aside plenty of time to watch it; perhaps plan a special evening when you can both relax and be absorbed back into the fun and frolics of your big day.

Changing your name

There is no legal reason for you to take your partner's name when you get married. If you do, the only paperwork you will need to verify your new name (for example, to apply for a new passport) is your marriage certificate. You can also choose to 'double-barrel' your surnames. You don't both have to use a new name, however if both of you do, you may be asked to produce formal evidence other than the marriage certificate.

It is more usual for the woman to take the man's name after marriage. If the reverse applies, the marriage certificate may be enough evidence to show that he has made that change, but he may also have to provide some other evidence. (Advice courtesy of www.clsdirect.org.uk.)

Civil partnership – name change

If you enter into a civil partnership you have four options:

- You and your partner can continue using your own names.
- One of you can change your name to the others.
- You can form a double-barrelled name.
- You can choose a new surname that you both use.

You should tell the registrar where your civil partnership will be registered if you or your partner would like to change your name. This should be done well in advance of the wedding. Usually, the registrar can put the correct names on your civil partnership certificate, which will then be evidence of the name change. However, in some cases the registrar may say that you should first obtain a deed poll. If this is the case, ensure that you apply for the deed poll at least three weeks before the ceremony. (Advice courtesy of www.clsdirect.org.uk.)

Making a will

Marriage

Your marriage will cancel out any previous wills and therefore it is advisable to make another will immediately following your wedding. An even better option is that you make a will 'in contemplation' of your marriage, which states that it will not be cancelled as you become man and wife. If you have made a will and then get divorced, the will stands true except for any bequests made to your ex-husband or wife which become void.

More advice can be found on the website www.advicenow.org.uk.

Intestacy

For civil partnerships

In accordance to the rules of intestacy, if you and your partner register your partnership and then one of you dies, the surviving partner inherits in the same way as a spouse, if there is no will.

After registering your partnership, you still need to make a will as any wills made beforehand will become void (as with marriage). You will then be recognized under the intestacy rules, and will benefit from the same exemption from inheritance tax as married couples. Before you register you can opt to amend any existing wills so they allow for the eventuality of a civil partnership, or you can simply have them amended afterwards.

Your civil partner will inherit under the rules governing intestate estates if you choose not to make a will, which will take into account children from existing or previous relationships. For further advice, visit www.stonewall.org.uk (Tel: 0207 593 1850), an organization dealing with gay/lesbian rights.

For couples not in civil partnerships

For those couples not in a civil partnership, a surviving partner could forfeit any claim on his or her partner's estate if a same-sex partner dies without leaving a will (intestate).

The laws of intestacy do not recognize 'unpartnered' survivors. Therefore if your partner dies intestate, their estate will go to your partner's parents or – if they are not living – to their siblings (if there are no siblings, then to remoter relatives). It is therefore clearly very important for lesbian or gay partners to make wills.

The only possible alternative for the remaining partner if there is no will, or no provision has been made for him or her, is to make a claim under the Inheritance (Provision for Family and Dependants) Act 1975. To do this it is necessary to show that you have been '... maintained, either wholly or partly by the deceased'. Where there has been an equal relationship in which both partners have contributed to their life together, it may not be possible to show dependence. One of the pieces of legislation that will be affected by the Mendoza judgement (see stonewall.org.uk) is that unmarried heterosexual partners living together as husband and wife do have a right to a claim on each other's estate.

Your wedding dress – store it or sell it?

Your wedding dress has been chosen with such love and affection that it would be a tragic shame to store it without consideration or care, which may lead to damage or deterioration over a period of time. It may become stained or discoloured and suffer permanent creasing and be spoilt forever which would be a terrible loss if you had hoped to hand it down as a family heirloom!

Storing your wedding dress

Joy Hepworth, proprietor of Memory Boxes in Nottingham, says: 'In our throwaway society it is important to try to preserve the past and I consider it very important to have memories to treasure and pass down to future generations.'

Factors that will affect the condition of the dress

Light: Direct exposure to both artificial and natural light can hinder the longevity of fabrics. Ultraviolet light is the most damaging type and causes the greatest degree of damage in the shortest time.

Temperature/humidity: These environmental factors are interconnected. Extremes in both temperature and humidity (moisture levels) can cause permanent damage. Moisture will encourage bacteria and insects and cause water staining on silk, and mould growth will occur when humidity levels are very high. If the temperature fluctuates fabrics can become discoloured.

Pests: Moths are a well-known hazard to garments, as are beetles, silverfish and mice.

Poor cleaning: If the gown has not been cleaned to a sufficiently high standard, stains such as perfume, perspiration, make-up and wine will create permanent marks.

Bad handling: The storage of gowns on hangers is not recommended. The dress may become misshapen and metal or wood hangers may increase acid pollution. Never hang the dress in a plastic slip cover as this is the worst medium for the wedding gown. The plastic chemicals react with the fabric causing excessive yellowing and tarnishing of white gowns and fading of coloured fabrics – the plastic is also a trap for moisture.

Wooden chests: Those made from natural wood have high acid content and will cause rapid deterioration and discoloration.

Acid-free storage boxes: Many suppliers will provide acid-free storage containers for wedding dresses. However, be wary of the styles which are decorated, printed or covered in fibrous paper, as this may eventually seep through into your dress. Also, do not use any colour other than white acid-free tissue to wrap the dress with; never blue or black. The box should protect against light and dust to reduce any risk of contamination.

Travel boxes: These boxes for carrying the wedding dress are lined with acid-free unbuffered (untreated) tissue to keep the gown in tip top condition until you safely reach your destination. They are specifically designed to fit comfortably in the overhead compartments of airplanes, so that brides are able to keep their precious garment with them at all times. They can even be made to fit the airline compartments that do not conform to a standard measurement.

These boxes are also available for the groom's waistcoat in order to preserve his clothing in perfect condition. They are also suitable for storing incredibly delicate and fragile vintage garments.

Selling your wedding dress

You may not be sentimental about your wedding gown and would prefer to put the profits of the sale of the dress to an item in your new home or use it to help celebrate your first anniversary! In this case, there are many ways of selling your dress (or buying a once-worn design for your big day). One popular avenue is the internet: there are many websites specializing in advertising once-worn wedding dresses in the UK and abroad. These sites will publish an advert of your dress and some will ask for photographs of the garment; it will be online for an agreed period of time. You will also be able to sell your bridesmaids' dresses by the same process.

Other options include Ebay, designer sales and advertising in the local and national press. Some wedding dress shops will take once-worn dresses from their collection and sell them on your behalf, taking a commission.

The art of compromise

According to marital research reports, 80 per cent of the things we argue about do not really need a solution. We just need to be able to talk about them. A marriage is about giving and taking and in order for it to progress successfully both spouses should practise the art of compromise.

It can happen that one spouse tends to compromise more than the other one. This hinders any chance of a successful, happy relationship because it promotes resentment in the spouse who is constantly having to give in and the festering of negative emotions is extremely destructive long-term. Try to take it in turns to ask questions and really listen to one another. If your spouse has a strong objection or feeling against something and you do not have a particular problem either way, consider your partner's feelings and say: 'This is obviously more important to you than it is to me. This time let's do it your way.' This will show your partner that you are willing to listen and hear their side and truly see the other person's perspective. Even when you disagree, in order to close the argument amicably, perhaps it would be wise to agree to disagree occasionally and keep the moment peaceful and calm, saving your real grievances for more important issues.

> 'Studies around the world confirm that passion usually ends; no wonder some cultures think that selecting a mate based on something so fleeting is folly. Long-term relationship commitment takes more than falling in love. Scientists are discovering that the cocktail of brain chemicals that sparks romance is totally different from the blend that fosters long-term attachment.'
>
> *National Geographic*, 2006

Senior writer Jeanie Learch Davis for WebMDHealth, says: 'Thermostat settings, dirty socks, toothpaste caps – our little habits make our spouses crazy! No two people are every truly compatible, so stop nitpicking each other. Save the battles for the big issues and you'll have a happy marriage.' John Gottman MD, psychologist and founder of The Gottman Institute in Seattle, US, says: 'Long-lasting happy marriages have more than great communication. Irreconcilable differences are normal and we should come to terms with them – try not to resolve the irresolvable. What is important is to be nice to each other – it is as simple as that! Make small gestures, but make them often – the little things matter! Knowing each other well, having mutual respect and learning how to identify issues that must be resolved and putting up with the rest are crucial. All you do is waste your breath and get angry over things that cannot be changed; work around them instead.'

For a happy marriage, says Terri Orbuch (award-winning Professor of Sociology), these are the ways of dealing with conflict:

- Bring it up in a non-threatening way. Be nice, no name calling. Bring up specific issues or behaviours, rather than personality qualities. You should not attack the person. Bring up the specific time, how you felt about it; then people can change the way they behave, otherwise they don't know what to do about it, they are boxed in. Use 'I' statements. Instead of 'You're a very messy person' say 'I am really bothered when you put the clothes on the floor.' Such statements show how you feel about a specific behaviour and that is important.
- Try to stay calm. Studies show that the calmer you are, the more you will be taken seriously. Take a breath, count to ten, breathe again. Take a break. If you are going back and forth, if you find the blood pressure going up, take a few seconds or minutes.
- Don't take hours! If you take too long, it festers in the other person and they have time to analyse it: you are dismissing their feelings, opinions and therefore dismissing them!
- Don't bring it up at night. Choose the right time – not when people are tired, hungry, when the children are around or when you have a deadline at work!
- Consider your spouse's point of view if you want a truly happy marriage. 'I'm a true believer of this,' says Orbuch. 'Studies show that every single action has a different meaning depending on if you are male, female, your race, your background. That is important to remember in conflict resolution. Direct meaningful communication is vital – but you have to choose the right time. One cannot feel that they are making all the compromises, it is uncomfortable for both – not just the one giving in. As long as in the long-term things are reciprocal, that is what matters.'

Darren Wilk, Registered Clinical Counsellor and Certified Gottman Therapist suggests: 'You will not compromise with someone until you feel like they accept you as you are. In great marriages there is a fascinating paradox happening all the time.

A spouse is able to present their ideas for change in such a way that the other person feels total acceptance yet also desires to change some things for their spouse.

'The way this is communicated is through the principle of Aikido: don't treat your spouse like an opponent but rather to join with them and see the problem from their perspective. Join them on their side of the problem and ask why their perspective is so important to them. What are all their feelings about? When you do this you gain empathy for them and you also disarm them: their defences will come down.

'The third thing to remember when compromising is to always share what you are not willing to give up first. Some small area that is too close to your core to give up. Something that feels like you would be betraying yourself to give in. When a person gives in on these areas the compromise is usually short-lived. After a non-negotiable is established the couple is much more relaxed in sharing areas that they are flexible on, regarding timing, place, amounts and other specifics.'

Keeping the passion alive!

Falling in love is easy. Staying in love and keeping the passion alive is another matter.

American life coach, Pamela Ramey-Tatum says: 'As a relationship coach, I often get asked if I really believe it is possible to keep passion alive in a long-term committed relationship or marriage. My answer is that, although it can be challenging, it's far from impossible. Like anything else worth having, it takes some time and attention to create a lasting relationship with a healthy amount of passion. You have to work at creating the magic; it won't just be there year after year if you don't.

'The day-to-day routine can actually build intimacy, rather than destroy it, if we make time to be intimate and giving with our partner every day. It's a choice, like the choice of allowing your partner's idiosyncrasies to make him or her more endearing to you rather than drive you crazy. The following are just a few of the things you can do to keep the fire burning between you and your long-term love:

- Remember to appreciate and savour the little pleasures, the bonuses of living together. Take time each day to connect intimately with your partner: deeply embrace and gaze into each other's eyes lovingly, feeling each other's energy. This can lead to sex or not, depending on your mood.

- Drift off in one another's arms; it's deeply satisfying. Even if you can't actually sleep that way, you can spend ten minutes or so embracing before moving apart to sleep. Then when you wake up, savour that time also, linger to spoon or embrace just a few more delicious moments before getting up.
- Spend some time together remembering how your relationship began, those first glances, dates, kisses – how you fell in love. Revisit some of the places where you had your 'firsts': first kiss, first date, initial attraction. This keeps those feelings of romantic love fresh and builds new positive memories as well.
- Have new and exciting experiences as often as you can. When you stay excited about exploring and experiencing life together, you stay more excited about each other too. So travel together, skinny dip, kayak, hike in the forest. Even small changes from your regular routine, such as going to a new restaurant or reading poetry together, can help rekindle the passion.
- Take a sacred sex workshop or some kind of intimacy-building workshop together. Or if money prohibits that, buy a book on the topic and practise some of the techniques together. Spicing things up in the bedroom can keep the sexual energy between you alive.
- Once a year do a retreat or vacation together, something that will nurture your souls or allow you to let loose and have fun. Ultimately, these kinds of experiences bring you closer together.
- Keep the energetic polarity between you. Women, worship the maleness of your partner, and men, worship the femaleness of your goddess woman. Women, learn to relax into your feminine essence and draw your man into your deliciousness. Then, let your man ravish you with his masculine energy.

'Though some people believe that living together kills the romance, seeing someone only for dating and sleepovers in a relationship that's never going to culminate in living together or marriage can lack deep intimacy. It has a sense of unreality about it. It's like being on vacation all the time. It sounds great but for most of us, it would get boring and shallow after a while.

'The real magic of a relationship is in the intimacy, and intimacy is built by sharing the good times and the bad, being there with each other everyday, experiencing the beautiful and the mundane, nurturing and loving each other through all of it. So living together doesn't have to kill the romance; just put a little work – or play – at keeping the passion alive.'

Passion workshops

As a fun way of sustaining or reviving a healthy sex life, couples are turning to salons offering workshops in a modern safe, relaxed environment to experiment and learn more about sexual pleasure. The concept dates back to the eighteenth century, where 'grande salons' played host to intellectual debate, music and debauchery. These contemporary workshops recreate this tradition of expressive freedom and encourage their clients to be open and honest with their feelings, with a view to improving their relationships and renewing love and passion in an exciting and stimulating way.

Wedding anniversaries

Your first wedding anniversary is a very special day and memories will come flooding back of your wedding day encompassing the emotions and excitement you felt together. It would be wonderful to take some time on your first anniversary to perhaps revisit your wedding venue or first night hotel and book yourselves into an evening of good food and wine and sumptuous, luxury accommodation to celebrate and relive the glamour of the day. Often the management of the venue or hotel where you were married will be delighted to arrange a special rate and offer an anniversary treat or two, so just ask and you should be pleasantly surprised at the response.

The gift you choose to give your new spouse on your wedding anniversary is usually based on the tradition of a different meaning for each year of marriage as follows, although some presents are easier to find and more appealing to receive than others!

Wedding anniversary gifts

1st	Paper
2nd	Cotton
3rd	Leather
4th	Linen
5th	Wood
6th	Iron
7th	Wool (copper)
8th	Bronze
9th	Pottery
10th	Tin/Aluminium
11th	Steel
12th	Silk
13th	Lace
14th	Ivory
15th	Crystal
20th	China
25th	Silver
30th	Pearl
35th	Coral/Jade
40th	Ruby
45th	Sapphire
50th	Gold

Renewing your vows

Renewing your wedding vows in front of friends and family is a ceremony that can occur any time after your original wedding, but is often chosen to celebrate on the tenth, fifteenth or twenty-fifth anniversary. There may be various reasons for choosing to organise such an event: often it is a celebration of a united couple, choosing to show that they are still happy in their marriage and want to publicly recommit themselves to one another. Alternatively, perhaps the couple have gone through some difficult times in their marriage and have reached the conclusion that they have successfully overcome the problems and challenges life has thrown them in which case they may be grateful for the second chance and feel that by reiterating their original vows, said when romance was new, that they will give a fresh lease of life to the years ahead and move on together as two individuals united by love.

The format can be similar to a religious wedding ceremony and take place in the church where you were married, and if the same priest or minister who married you is available, he will be happy to discuss the ceremony with you repeating many of the original wording and he will be able to make suggestions for a choir, hymns or readings. Couples who have had children may relish the opportunity of including their youngsters in the service, and any other family or friends who may want to do a reading or make a brief address to the congregation about the couple and their life together so far.

If married in a civil ceremony, you may prefer to write your own vows and have a less formal event, with the ceremony held in your garden, or at the original wedding venue. It is basically a good excuse for a party, buying a new outfit and inviting close members of your family and friends to share a special day with you. Rings are not usually exchanged, however, if a new anniversary ring has been bought, for the wife, or for each other, this would be the perfect time to receive it from your devoted spouse! The day can be as simple or as elaborate as you wish, including details such as playing your wedding video in the background and having your wedding photographs on display for guests to glance through and reminisce. Whatever way you choose to celebrate the renewal of your vows, just simply being able to take the time to remember your wedding day and cherish the moment you declared your love for each other, will be truly beneficial in promoting a stronger, happier relationship for many years to come.

Finale

I hope this book has been helpful in your quest to achieve your dream wedding day! If you use the information and advice to arrange a uniquely memorable (and relatively stress-free) wedding, it will be successful and provide you with the tools to forge ahead with your plans in a confident, informed way: knowing that you are able to ask all the right questions, check every angle and avoid any potential disappointing episodes in the run up to your big day.

With the wedding over, a new and exciting phase is beginning in your lives. I wish you health, happiness and good luck in your future together. Cherish one another.

> 'Stand together, yet not too near each other, for in the garden of life, the oak tree and the cypress each have air to breathe and a little earth to call their own, where the sun can reach down and touch them bringing forth the hidden beauty that lies within each one. Yes, be together, and be yourself. Be free, and always be together.'
>
> *The Prophet*, Kahil Gibran

Useful organizations

General Register Office
Marriages & Civil Partnerships Section
Trafalgar Road
Southport
PR8 2HH
Tel: 0151 471 4814
www.gro.org.uk

Changing your name
www.clsdirect.org.uk

Church of England
www.cofe.anglican.org.uk

Making a will
www.advicenow.org.uk
www.stonewall.org.uk

Society of Humanists
www.humanism.org.uk

Scottish Humanist society
www.humanism-scotland.org.uk

Useful suppliers

Asian weddings
www.Tania-tapel.com
Tel: 0116 247 1115

Balloons

Balloon decoration:
Balloon and Kite
613 Garratt Lane
London
SW18 4SU
Tel: 0208 946 5962
www.balloonandkite.com

Hot air balloons:
Bailey Balloons
44 Ham Green
Bristol
BS20 OHA
Tel: 01275 375 300
www.baileyballoons.co.uk

Bars
40A Holmethorpe Avenue
Redhill
Surrey
RH1 2NL
Tel: 01737 210979
www.bashbars.co.uk

Bespoke tailoring
Norton and Townsend
111 Canon Street
London
EC4N 5AR
Tel: 0207 929 5662
www.nortonandtownsend.co.uk

Beverages
Cocktail Heaven
66 Upper Road
London
E13 ODH
Tel: 0208 548 4022
www.createcocktails.com

Cakes
Meadow Cottage
Homington Road
Coombe Bissett
Salisbury
Wiltshire
SP5 4ND
Tel: 01722 718518
www.lindafripp.com

www.choccywoccydoodah.com

Cake sculpture
Roydon Fen
Roydon
Diss
Norfolk
Tel: 01379 643995
www.kathyscott.co.uk

Caterers
63–65 Goldney Road
London
W9 2AR
Tel: 0207 286 1600
www.urbancaprice.co.uk

Catering equipment hire
24 Creekside
Deptford
London
SE8 3DZ
Tel: 0208 320 0600
www.joneshire.co.uk
www.rayners.co.uk

Children's art and craft activities
www.arty-animals.com
Tel: 0208 682 0386

Children's party bags
www.littleangelbags.com
Tel: 01923 712278

Chocolate fountains
www.theoriginalchocolatefountain.com

Civil partnership weddings
Pad 108
15 Church Street
Weybridge
Surrey
KT13 8AN
www.pinkweddings.eu

Civil Partnership Stationery
www.timbershackcards.co.uk
www.pinkproducts.co.uk

Commission a poem
The Poetry Studio
1 Marlborough Mews
Court Road
Banstead
Surrey
SM7 2GJ
www.thepoetrystudio.co.uk
Tel: 01737 357900

Confetti
www.passionforpetals.com
01404 4811467

Favours
www.coxandcox.co.uk
Tel: 0870 442 4787

Fireworks
Phoenix Fireworks
Hill Park Farm
Wrotham Hill Road
Wrotham
Near Sevenoaks
Kent
TN15 7PX
Tel: 0845 680 0865
www.phoenixfireworks.co.uk

First night stays
www.rowtoncastle.com
www.downhall.co.uk
www.flemings.co.uk
www.dukeshotel.com
www.gilpinlodge.co.uk
www.carton.ie

Florists
Mary Jane Vaughan
609 Fulham Road
London
SW6 5UA
Tel: 0207 385 8400
www.fastflowers.co.uk
www.wildatheart.com

Gifts
Gift lists:
www.johnlewisgiftlist.com
www.wrapit.co.uk

Charity gift lists:
www.oxfamunwrapped.com
www.thealternativeweddinglist.co.uk
www.greatweddings.org

Alternative gifts:
www.redletterdays.co.uk

Hat stands
www.standingpretty.co.uk
Tel: 07722 602027

Headdresses
1C Kensington Church Walk
London W8 4NB
Tel: 0207 937 5115
www.isabelkurtenbach.com

Honeymoon destinations
www.manoir.com
www.inverlochycastlehotel.com
www.lucknampark.co.uk
www.longuevillemanor.com
www.domainedesandeols.com
www.the-valley.co.uk
www.southwestwalksireland.com
www.sixsenses.com
www.piccololago.com

Insurance
E & L Insurance
Thorpe Underwood Hall
Thorpe Underwood
Ouseburn
York
YO26 9SS
Tel: 08449 809565
www.e&linsurance.co.uk

Make-up stylist
www.elleaunaturel.com
Tel: 01737 249 844

Marquees
LPM Bohemia
Kent
TN12 8DP
Tel: 0870 770 7185
www.lpmbohemia.com

Marriage counselling/relationship coach
www.bestmarriage.com
www.empoweringlove.com
www.gottman.com

Menswear
Anthony Formal Wear
53 High Street
Billericay
Essex
CM12 9AX
Tel: 01277 651140
www.anthonyformalwear.co.uk

Music
Entertainment agencies:
Sternberg Clarke
140 Wandsworth High Street
London
SW18 4JJ
Tel: 0208 877 1102
www.sternbergclarke.co.uk

Music for the ceremony:
www.weddingsongs.co.uk
Tel: 01753 882646

Gospel choir:
www.lcgc.org.uk
Tel: 0208 509 7288

Photographers
www.juliaboggiophotography.com
Tel: 07712 531645

Dave Waller
4 Hampden Crescent
Warley
Brentwood
Essex
CM14 5BD
Tel: 01277 849184
www.davewaller.co.uk

www.theodorewood.com

Production and design
www.junoproductions.co.uk

Selling your wedding dress
www.thedressmarket.net
Tel: 0800 052 1465
www.almostnewweddingdresses.co.uk

Stag and hen parties
www.spy-games.com
Tel: 08451 303007

Stationery
www.wrenpress.co.uk
www.cleartouch.co.uk

Storing your wedding dress
Memory Boxes
PO Box 9164
Marchant
Nottingham
NG4 9BJ
Tel: 01636 830108
www.memoryboxes.co.uk

Tour operators
Sandals Holidays
36 Ives Street
London
SW3 2ND
Tel: 0800 742742
www.sandalsholidays.co.uk

Transport
www.bigredbuswedding.com
Tel: 0845 2575271

www.gleneaglescds.co.uk

www.thelimopeople.co.uk

www.weddingtaxis.co.uk
Tel: 08701 994251

Venues – London
www.londoneye.com
www.madametussauds.com
www.thegundocklands.com
www.landmarklondon.co.uk
www.barbican.org.uk
www.goldenhinde.org.uk
www.silverfleet.co.uk
www.crowneplaza.co.uk
www.theconservatoryvenue.co.uk

Venues – Country
www.countryhouseweddings.co.uk
www.thornburycastle.co.uk
www.monkeyisland.co.uk
www.bathvenues.co.uk
www.ravensait.co.uk
www.dodevillage.com

Video film makers
www.thegrahamfentonexperience.com
Tel: 01253 884100

www.theweddingdocumentarycompany.com
Tel: 01787 881463/0771 0611368

Weddings abroad
www.weddingsmadeinitaly.co.uk
Tel: 01424 728901

www.montecarloweddings.com
Tel: 377 935 03595

www.ultimateusaweddings.com

Empire State Building
350 Fifth Avenue Suite 5520
New York
NY 10118
USA
Tel: 212 563 3525

index

accessories **96–8**
after dinner novelties **120–1**
afternoon tea menu **110**
age, minimum legal **42**
agencies, entertainment **146–7**
aisle runners **84**
anniversaries **188–9**
announcements **2**
Antonia **100**
Asian wear **103**
Asian Wedding Show **26**
Asian weddings **52–4, 165**

balloons
  for decoration **83, 114**
  hot air **166**
bands, music **145, 149–50**
Banns, publication of **33**
bar hire **116**
best man **4–6, 102, 126**
Bewick, Emma **74**
Bible readings **37–40**
birthstone chart **3**
Boggio, Julia **139, 140**
booking, suppliers **27–8**
bouquets **xiv, 124–5, 129**
bridal magazines **31, 62**
bridal party **4–9**
bridesmaids **7–8, 125**
buses, London double decker **166**
buttonholes **126**

cake stands **112, 117**
cake tops **117–18**
cakes **17, 53, 116–19, 128**
cameras **84, 89, 114**
  see also photographs
Caribbean weddings **50–1, 68–9**
carriages **164–5**
cars **133, 162–4**
caterers **17, 105–9**
Catholic church **35–6, 156**
ceremonies
  church **33–41**
  civil **41–6**
  fees **16**
chairs **77, 107**
champagne fountains **120**
charity gift lists **91**
chief bridesmaid **6–7**
children, entertaining **158–9**
chocolate fountains **119**
chocolates **120**
choirs **151**
church ceremonies **33–41**
church music **151–6**
Church of England ceremony **33–5**
civil ceremonies **41–6, 156–7**
civil partnerships **46–8, 87–8, 180, 181**
clothes **16, 94–103**
cocktails **115**
Common Licence **34–5**
compromise, art of **184–6**
confetti **78, 80–1, 132–3**
costs **16–17**
country weddings **60**
crockery **78–9, 106**

cultural traditions **xvii–xix, 53**
customs **xii–xix, 53**
cutlery **106**
cutting of the cake **118**

Damgaard, Frank **68**
dance lessons **148**
dates, choosing **19–20**
decorations
  table **78–9**
  venue **72–5**
Designer Wedding Show **26**
dietary traditions **53**
discotheques **146**
dresses **16, 94–6, 182–3**
drinks **17, 114–16**

engagements **2–4**
entertainment
  for children **158–9**
  fireworks **159–160**
  musical during ceremony **145–50**
etiquette, of speeches **10**
event companies **74–7**
'experience days' **92**

father of the bride **8–9, 102, 126**
favours **80, 81–3**
  see also novelties
Fenton, Jane **142**
financial considerations **16–17**
financial responsibility **10**
fire engines **166**
firework displays **159–60**
first night stays **17, 170–1**
fitness **30**
florists **123–4**
flowers **16, 113, 123–33**
food **17, 105, 107–8, 109–10**
foreign nationals **34, 52**
Francoise, Catherine **151, 155**
French weddings **68**
Fripp, Linda **119**
furniture **77–8, 107**

gay weddings **46–8**
gift lists **90–2**
gifts
  after dinner **120–1**
  for attendants **16**
  for mother of the bride/groom **128**
  wedding **179**
  wedding anniversary **189**
  see also favours; novelties
glassware **78–9, 106**
good luck omens **xiv**
Gottman, John **184**
graces (prayers) **40–1**
Graffi studio coffee table books **141**
groom **126**
guest books **89, 114**

hairstyles **98–9**
hats **97–8**
headdresses **16, 97, 125**
health **30**
Hebborn, Father William **37**
hen parties **13–14**
Hepworth, Joy **182**
hire, of menswear **102–3**
honeymoons
  average cost **17**
  destinations **171–3**
  preparation **173–7**
horse and carriage **164–5**
hot air balloons **166**
hotels **110–14**
Howard, Alan **141, 143**
Humanist blessing **48–9**
hymns **151–4**

ice sculptures **84**
Indian weddings **52–4**
insurance **28–30, 174**
internet **61–2**
intestacy **181**
invitations **86–8, 90**
Italian weddings **66–7**
itinerary **21**

journey, to ceremony **xiii–xiv, 162–8**

kisses, ceremonial **xvi**
Kurten Bach, Isabel **97**

Learch Davis, Jeanie **184**
licences

common **34–5**
special **34**
lighting **75–7**
limousines **163**
'line-ups' **12**
linen **78, 106**

magazines **31, 62, 123**
maid/matron of honour **6–7**
make-up **99–100**
marquees **63–5**
marrying abroad **50–2, 66–70**
Master of Ceremonies **12**
menswear **101–3**
menus **88, 107–8, 111, 113**
Meriano, Gino and Mike **47**
mother of the bride **8, 128**
music
church **151–6**
civil ceremonies **156–7**
reception **145–50**

names, changing **174, 179–80**
National Wedding Show **26**
New York weddings **69–70**
Notice of Marriage **41–2**
novelties **120–1**
see also favours

Orbuch, Terri **185**
Order of Service sheets **88**
Order of the Day sheets **88**
organic food **109–10**
organists **151**
outfits **16, 94–103**

packing **176–7**
pageboys **8, 102, 126**
parish priests **36–7**
parties, stag and hen **13–14**
passion, keeping alive **186–8**
passports **174**
Patel, Anita **52**
photographers **135–40**
photographs **3, 16, 84, 89, 135–41, 179**
Pink Weddings **47**
place cards **79–80, 88, 113**
place settings **79**
planners, professional **17–18**
planners, year **21–4**
poems **46**
pre-canna sessions **36–7**
preparation classes **36–7**
Preston, Charles **65**
priests **36–7**
publication of the Banns **33**

Ramey Tatum, Pamela **186**
readings
Bible **37–40**
civil ceremony **42–6**
receiving lines **12**
register offices **63**
reply cards **88**
resort weddings **50–1**
rings **xvi, 3, 16, 24**

'save the date' cards **86–7**
Scooby Doo van **165**
Scott, Kathy **118**
Scottish Wedding Show **26**
Scottish weddings **61**
seating plans **11–12, 79–80, 89**
second marriages **49**
shoes **xiii–xiv, 16**
shows, wedding **25–7**
Society of Humanists **48**
songs **151–4**
special dietary requirements **106**
special licence **35**
speeches **9–10**
staffing **108**
stag parties **13–14**
stationery **16, 86–9**
Sternberg, Adam **147**
stress **31**
styles *see* themes
suit hire **102–3**
suppliers, booking **27–8**

table decorations **78–9**
table plans **113**
tablecloths **78, 106**
tables **77–8, 107**
theatrical weddings **59**
themes **72–5**
Thornton-Allan, Lizzie **120**

timetable **20–1**
see also year planner
top tables **11–12**
tour operators **50–1, 69**
town weddings **58–9**
traditions **xii–xix, 53**
transport **16, 162–8**
travel insurance **174**
Turnbull, Matthew **109**

ushers **102, 126**

Vaughan, Mary Jane **123**
veils **xiii**
venues
abroad **50–2, 66–70**
average cost **17**
for civil ceremonies **41**
country **60**
marquees **63–5**
selecting **56–8**
sources of information **61–2**
styling and decorating **72–5**
town **58–9**
videos **16, 141–3, 179**
vintage cars **162–3**
vows, renewing **189–90**

weather forecasts **65–6**
wedding cakes **17, 53, 116–19, 128**
wedding dresses **16, 94–6, 182–3**
wedding nights **170–1**
wedding packages **110–14**
wedding planners **17–18**
wedding shows **25–7**
Wedding Venues & Services magazine **62**
weddings abroad **50–2, 66–70**
Wilk, Darren **185**
wills **180–1**
World Vision **91**

Yates, Andrew **83**
year planner **21–4**
yurts **65**